Book Design: Pierce Centina
Art Consultant: Janet Frances White

This edition first published in 2023 by Centiramo Publishing
New York, NY • www.centiramopublishing.com

The Independent History of Ylongo and Cebuano Visayans © 2023 by Guillermo Gómez Rivera. All rights reserved. No part of this publication may be reproduced, distributed, or transmitted in any form or by any means, including photocopying, recording, or other electronic or mechanical methods, without the prior written permission of the publisher, except in the case of brief quotations embodied in critical reviews and certain other noncommercial uses permitted by copyright law. For permission requests, write to the publisher, addressed "Attention: Permissions Coordinator" at info@centiramopublishing.com.

The Internet links provided in this book were active during the time of its publication. However, due to the constantly changing nature of the World Wide Web, the publisher cannot guarantee the continued availability of these links over time.

This book employs Filipino and Spanish words without italicization, as they are commonly known by its primary audience, who are predominantly Filipino readers.

ISBN: 13-978-1-958406-03-8
ISBN: 10-1-958406-03-1

Library of Congress Control Number: 2022947067
LC record available at https://lccn.loc.gov/2018960697

Printed in the United States of America

3 5 7 9 11 13 15 17 19 | 20 18 16 14 12 10 8 6 4 2

THE INDEPENDENT HISTORY OF YLONGO AND CEBUANO VISAYANS

by
GUILLERMO GÓMEZ RIVERA

DEDICATION

With heartfelt gratitude, I dedicate this book to my beloved family and to my fellow Ylongos, who share with me the ability to speak Ylongo-Hiligaynon but also have a fondness for reading in the English language. Your unwavering support and encouragement have been invaluable in bringing this work to fruition, and it is my hope that it will serve as a meaningful contribution to our shared cultural heritage.

Contents

Dedication: V
Prologue: XI
Preface: XIII

CHAPTER I
Rizal As Our House Guest In Iloilo City: 2

CHAPTER II
The Legendary Teniente Guimó: 16

CHAPTER III
Teniente Guimó's Dueñas Forebears: 24

CHAPTER IV
The Need For An Independent History: 30

CHAPTER V
Real Benevolence: Spanish Citizenship: 38

CHAPTER VI
Why Visayans Sided With Spain: 44

CHAPTER VII
Ylongos Shunned 'Masonic' Katipunan: 50

CHAPTER VIII
Inventing Heroes To Confuse History: 64

CHAPTER IX
Spain Says 'Adios' To Loyal Ylongos: 70

CHAPTER X
Anti-Spanish Manila Should Be Opposed: 76

Contents

CHAPTER XI
How Ylongos Viewed Rizal, KKK Leaders: *84*

CHAPTER XII
The Damaging 'Inglisero' Culture: *90*

CHAPTER XIII
Invented Language Is Ruining Our Culture: *96*

CHAPTER XIV
The Intellectual Deficiency of Puristas: *106*

CHAPTER XV
The Race To Protect Ylongo Identity: *114*

CHAPTER XVI
Epic Reveals Advanced Pre-Hispanic Culture: *118*

CHAPTER XVII
Villa De Arévalo: Iloilo's First Spanish Pueblo: *126*

CHAPTER XVIII
The Root Of Rizal's Anti-Friar Writings: *132*

CHAPTER XIX
Revising History To Serve Neocolonialism: *140*

CHAPTER XX
Can We Trust America's 'Strategic Ambiguity'?: *146*

CHAPTER XXI
Visayan Sense Of Unity Remains Unshakable: *152*

CHAPTER XXII
How Large-Scale Corruption Started: *156*

Contents

CHAPTER XXIII
Classic Ylongo Poetry Is True To Spanish Form: *166*

CHAPTER XXIV
Priceless Childhood Memories Recalled: *176*

CHAPTER XXV
The Hispanic Culture of Cebu: *184*

CHAPTER XXVI
Extraordinary Citizens Drive Iloilo Forward: *200*

Epilogue: *207*
Photographic Credits: *210*
Index: *212*

PROLOGUE

GUILLERMO GÓMEZ RIVERA

Un hispanista, he is Don Quijote,
Sancho Panza without *sombrero*;
The insular combination of both,
Un gran hispanista de las islas filipinas,
He is the memento of *Madre España,*
The Conundrum of Gibraltar,
The Passion of the flamenco,
Faith in *El Cristo de Velázquez,*
Mystery in Goya's *Maja Desnuda,*
Defiance in Picasso's *Guernica,*
Amor y pedagogía de Unamuno,
El Escorial de Felipe II:
La suerte en la corrida de toros.

Un hispanista, he can be El Cid
When, armed only with a laptop,
He gallops Rosinante to the battlefield
To wipe out vestiges of *leyendas negras,*
As Dulcinea, adorned with rubies and gold,
Dances the *paso doble* with lissome *bailadoras.*

—*Gilbert Luis R. Centina III*

PREFACE

THE INDEPENDENT HISTORY OF YLONGO AND CEBUANO VISAYANS   XIII

Iloilo is experiencing a renaissance with its thriving economy and modern infrastructure. The city has witnessed the emergence of sparkling new buildings, excellent roads, bridges, highways, and a plethora of appealing commercial centers. Tourists are drawn to Iloilo due to its ubiquitous malls, the annual Dinagyang religious-cultural festival, revived cuisine, and the preservation of its historical landmarks.

The city's new leaders, including Senator Franklin Drilon, Governors Neil Tupas and Arthur Defensor Jr., Mayors Jerry Treñas and José Espinosa, and others, have successfully brought about these positive transformations. Iloilo has regained its position as a center of politics, commerce, education, industry, and culture in Western Visayas under their leadership.

As the older generation fades away, it is the responsibility of the new generations to embrace their Ylongo-Hiligaynon heritage and ensure it is not lost. To achieve this goal, the immediate task is to liberate the Ylongo-Hiligaynon language from the limitations of abakadization and restore it to its Spanish-Binisaya traditions based on the original *La Panayana* librettos and tracts.

To this end, efforts should be directed toward rejuvenating traditional Spanish dances that have lost their charm over the years, the local fiesta spirit, and the parián (marketplace) traditions that were prevalent during the Spanish era.

Furthermore, it is important to reignite the people's interest in the Spanish language, which was once widely spoken in the city and is a significant storehouse of the country's history.

In light of the present situation, there is an imperative need to revive the old ancestral houses on Calle Santo Rosario that were destroyed in the name of progress. Regrettably, these grand ancestral residences, numbering three or four from our recollection, were demolished to make way for the now somewhat outdated Government Service Insurance System (GSIS) building, with little consideration for their cultural value. With contemporary amenities, these structures could be reconstructed as replicas. This concept could give rise to a novel cultural heritage site, coexisting with GSIS in harmony, surrounded by Spanish-style cantinas, tiendecitas, and eateries for all to appreciate.

We believe that the Rizal monument in Plaza Libertad should be replaced with one commemorating General Martín Teófilo Delgado, who played a significant role in the country's struggle for independence, particularly against the United States. Additionally, the umbrella-shaped lamp post monument at Plazoleta Gay ought to be restored, as the phallic-shaped structure that replaced it offends people's sensibilities. Moreover, we suggest relocating the new Chinese arch, which stands between the old Celso Ledesma Building and the antiquated Serafin-Anita Villanueva Arcade across Iznart and Ledesma streets, to the entrance of Molo or the approach to the new Iloilo River Bridge and Esplanade near the SM Mall.

It is essential to reconstruct Fort San Pedro, La Cotta, and beautify the drive from the Laguda ruins to Calle Durán's tip near the old Casino Español. The historically significant Casino Español should be restored as a Spanish-style mansion or boutique hotel, complete with a dance school and specialty shops. Moreover, the run-down houses at the other end of Calle Durán should be renovated in the balay nga bato kag tapi (wood and stone house) style.

To educate young Ylongos about their glorious past, we have included glimpses of Iloilo's history in the 1890s and 1900s in this book. Also discussed are the legendary Teniente Guimó, a sorcerer hero, and the now-forgotten Batallón Ylongo de Voluntarios and Batallones de Cebuanos Leales. These groups wisely sided with Spain against the Tagalog Katipuneros, who were a virtual fifth column of the invading Americans. The Voluntarios, led by General Delgado, only joined General Emilio Aguinaldo after peacefully gaining independence from the Spanish forces in Iloilo. As per the Treaty of Paris, the Spanish government ordered its armed forces to leave the Philippines.

We also address the Tagalog Abakada-Balarila purista colonization of Iloilo schoolchildren, resulting in rising linguistic and cultural illiteracy among children. According to a World Bank report, "nine out of 10 Filipino children...are unable to read" (*Philippine Daily Inquirer,* November 21, 2021 issue). This educational deficit can be traced back to the elimination of the Spanish Abecedario from Tagalog and other native languages, including Ylongo-Hiligaynon. Spanish language teaching was also abolished from the country's educational system. Learning philosophy, physics, mathematics, and other classical Western concepts becomes challenging in an Abakada-driven classroom.

We hold that teaching Spanish in schools can significantly improve students' learning, considering that English and Spanish already share sixty-five percent of vocabulary cognates. We also discuss how to repair the grave linguistic, cultural, political, and economic damage inflicted upon the estimated fifteen million Ylongos by the pernicious Tagalog Abakada-Balarila colonization. This systematic uprooting has negatively impacted the Spanish heritage of even the true Tagalogs, resulting in the cultural destruction of the Tagalogs in various ways.

We urge non-Tagalog Filipinos who share Spanish heritage, such as the Ylongo-Hiligaynons, to take positive steps to defend their cultural identity against the ongoing Tagalog purista language colonization. The Spanish national heritage is a pillar of their identity and development, and they must unite to preserve it.

In addition to the history and cultural analysis, the book also features Hiligaynon poems and personal memories of our social milieu and family. Writing this book is a tribute to the people who have shaped our life. The memories and accounts shared in the book aim to help young people appreciate their past.

G.G.R., Makati City
March 22, 2023

Chapter 1
RIZAL AS OUR HOUSE GUEST IN ILOILO CITY

When José Rizal returned to Manila from his Dapitan exile, his steamer made a stopover in Iloilo City. Early in the morning, after his vessel had safely docked, he disembarked and went straight to Plaza Alfonso XII (now Plaza Libertad) to inquire about the address of his close friend Emilio Villanueva y Felipe from a well-known botica located at the corner of Calle Progreso and Calle Real. Emilio, now a lawyer, was part of Rizal's pandilla-barcada in Madrid in the 1880s, where they both attended the same university. Once he found out where the Villanueva mansion was, Rizal asked the boticario about the location and distance of Molo.

He planned to spend the night at the Villanueva mansion and sent word for Emilio to come and get him. Rizal paid a cochero, recommended by the same boticario, to drive to Molo and inform Don Emilio about his brief stay in la Ciudad de Iloilo.

While Rizal was sitting in the botica, my grandfather, Felipe Gómez y Windham, walked in and saw him. At that time, my grandfather was a young man who had read about the famous eye doctor and novelist. He approached Rizal and introduced himself. Rizal greeted him with a smile and started a conversation. However, Felipe had to cut it short since he was there on an errand to pick up medications for his father, Doctor José María Gómez de Arce. Felipe excused himself, promising Rizal he would be back soon since his home was just a short walk across the plaza. In less than half an hour, my grandfather returned to resume his chat with Rizal.

※

DON EMILIO ARRIVED at the botica entrance in his elegant carruaje, driven by his cochero, past nine in the morning. After alighting from the carruaje, Don Emilio warmly embraced Rizal, as if reuniting with a long-lost brother. He then requested a table from the formally dressed boticario as the establishment doubled as a Spanish restaurant and bazaar, similar to a modern-day department store.

Being a scion of the financially prominent Villanueva clan from the opulent Sector de Mestizos or Parián de Molo, Don Emilio ordered refreshments and Spanish dishes fit for royalty. He invited José and Felipe to join him at the table.

After enjoying some Spanish red wine and a delicious mid-morning second breakfast, Don Emilio apologetically informed Rizal that he could not accommodate him in his house. His mother, a Spanish mestiza from Bicol, was strongly

In the center of Plaza Libertad, there stands a statue of Rizal, with San José Parish Church visible in the background. An inset photo shows the same plaza, dating back to circa 1907.

against it. Having been awarded the Pro Ecclesia et Pontifice medal, Doña María Felipe de Villanueva did not want anything to do with a Mason like Rizal, let alone host him at her residence. She considered it "buisit," a Fukien-Ua word which means "no food available to eat," or simply bad luck.

The leading Filipino families in Iloilo felt this hostility because they considered themselves loyal Spanish citizens and subjects. The Masons were looked down upon as traitors to Spain and its overseas territories, including the Philippines. Furthermore, the Manila authorities suspected them of spying for the anti-Catholic White Anglo-Saxon Protestant North American power with imperialistic ambitions. The rising world power was already gearing up for an expansionist territorial war against Spain and its overseas possessions such as the Philippines, Cuba, Puerto Rico, and Guam. This perceived threat was not limited to Manila alone, as it concerned even the peace-loving Ylongos in the middle of the country.

Doña María did not want any trouble, either with God Almighty or her Spanish King.

HER FAMILY AND FRIENDS shared the anti-Mason sentiment prevalent among the Visayan chinos cristianos who owned vast haciendas. They feared being associated with the banned organization under Spanish law, as it could jeopardize their social and financial status as landowners, merchants, and traders. Don Emilio's mother, a papal awardee, had read about the allegedly anti-Catholic leaflets found in Rizal's luggage, which had led to his exile to Dapitan four years earlier in 1892. Insulting the Catholic Church was unacceptable to her.

As Rizal listened to Don Emilio's explanation, Felipe, our grandfather and a Mason like his father, smiled wryly. To resolve the situation, Felipe invited Rizal to stay at his family's house, the Gómez-Windham mansion.

Don Emilio expressed his gratitude to our grandfather for saving him from an awkward situation. In his eagerness to make amends, he generously offered to cover Rizal's food expenses by requesting the boticario to send meals to the Gómez-Windham residence. He even added a generous tip for the servers involved in the delivery, paying for it with bills from the Banco Español-Filipino de Isabel II de las Islas Filipinas, which was commonly known as Banco Islas at that time.

Following their delightful almuerzo, Don Emilio took José and Felipe on a tour of Calle Real in the city and the suburbs of Molo. During their visit to Molo, they paused at a house with windows overlooking the Iloilo saltwater river, which Spanish-speaking Ylongos referred to as "ría," to admire the stunning view. They also visited the local church, strolled around Plaza de Molo, and marveled at the opulent principalía houses in the población before returning to the city proper.

Overall, Don Emilio proved to be a gracious host who showed José and Felipe some of the area's most beautiful sights and historical landmarks. They started their journey by passing the impressive Casa Real at the start of Calle Iznart, then made their way to the muelle to collect Rizal's luggage from the ship docked at the estuary. In 1904, the city council officially named the wharf Muelle Loney in honor of Nicholas Loney, a British businessman who later became the British

The Ynchausti Commercial House on Calle Real, now known as the Iloilo Economic History Museum, is the first museum of its kind in the country.

This photo, captured in the early twentieth century, portrays Calle Real, the main street in Iloilo City, as it would have appeared to Rizal during his visit to the city.

vice-consul in Iloilo. Loney played a crucial role in modernizing the Philippine sugar industry during the 1860s. The wharf was the site of the Iloilo Customs House and remains so today.

Next, they headed to the Gómez-Windham mansion, located beside the main city square, Plaza Alfonso XII, and the San José Parish Church. There, Rizal met Doctor Gómez, who was the city's sanitary physician and the military doctor of the old Fort San Pedro, known as La Cotta in Spanish or kuta in Hiligaynon.

During their conversation, Rizal discovered that Doctor Gómez had a Batangueña grandmother named María Nelia Dimaculañgan, who was pure Tagalog and the wife of his peninsular grandfather, Francisco Gómez Monfort. The Gómez-Dimaculañgan family had twelve children who were born in Pagsanjan. One of them, Fernando, was sent to Spain to study and ended up marrying a pure española from Navarra and Madrid named De Arce. Doctor Gómez' Spanish roots motivated him to Hispanize his wife's British last name from Wyndham to Windham.

Dolores' father held the position of acting British consul. William Wyndham, later known as Guillermo Windham after his conversion to Catholicism, was an Anglican and a Mason. He married Rosario, a mestiza from the Locsin-Araneta clan. Dolores Windham de Gómez, their daughter, gave birth to two sons, Felipe, our grandfather, and Guillermo, our granduncle, who became a renowned Ylongo writer in Spanish.

During the American occupation of Iloilo City, Felipe and Guillermo, who briefly studied in British Hong Kong, were hired by the American invaders as interpreters and assistants, as only a few people in Iloilo knew English at that time.

Don Emilio Villanueva y Felipe

Felipe was appointed as the mayor and police chief of Iloilo, while Guillermo became a Customs inspector in Iloilo and later in Manila. After his retirement in 1945, he served as a war damage commissioner for the Quirino administration.

※

RIZAL CONFIDED IN Doctor Gómez, his sons, and Dolores about his legal troubles and the true reason behind his animosity toward the Spanish friars. The Dominican friars had filed an ejectment case against Rizal, his brother Paciano, and their family, which they ultimately lost after the Royal Audiencia ruled against them. Despite the family's argument that questioned Dominican ownership of the haciendas in Calamba and Los Baños, which the friars leased to them, the court affirmed their eviction for non-payment of rent. Although this argument delayed the case for years, their lawyer eventually dropped it as it had no legal basis. Guillermo, who had knowledge of the law, cautioned Rizal against escalating the matter by even questioning Spanish ownership of the entire archipelago, which Rizal had expressed in his writings.

Rizal's resentment toward the friars was evident in his literary works, particularly in his zarzuela *Junto al Pasig*, where he used the devil's character to express his feelings against the child protagonist, Leonido.

Doctor Gómez and his sons assisted Rizal in formulating his defense in case of a court trial for treason by reviewing his writings that could be used against him. They correctly predicted that the authorities would charge Rizal with the crime soon. Felipe advised Rizal to leave the country while he still could and stay out of circulation until the political atmosphere had cooled down, allowing local Spanish authorities to be more forgiving of his alleged offenses.

Rizal arrived in Iloilo on August 4, 1896, and was executed by a firing squad on December 30 that year for treason and alleged association with the Masonic Katipunan. Since their community leaders and leading businessmen and landowners were already wary of the Katipunan, it was not hard for the rest of the Ylongo and Cebuano populations to reject the group, seeing it as a subversive Tagalog organization funded by the anti-Spanish American Masons.

Don Felipe Gómez y Windham

FILIPINAS AND CUBA were prosperous nations, blessed with natural resources such as sugar, tobacco, and valuable minerals, and were economically stable even without borrowing money from American banks or monetary lending institutions. However, the United States desired their resources and instigated a war against Spain, which was already weakened, to seize its overseas territories and transform them into dependent states.

After the Pact of Biacnabató put an end to the Filipino revolution against Spain, and Aguinaldo went into exile in Hong Kong, the American war against Spain shifted to a conflict with Aguinaldo's República de Filipinas.

In Cuba, the United States controlled the country's economic and political affairs until Fidel Castro overthrew its puppet government under Fulgencio Batista, leading to a successful revolution. However, this also resulted in the imposition of a U.S. embargo against Cuba in 1962, which has persisted to this day, crippling the Cuban economy for over half a century. This embargo is merely a continuation of the aggression against Spain and its overseas territories during the nineteenth century.

AS A RESPONSE to the Americans' threat of war against Spain, the Ylongos established and financed their own Batallón de Voluntarios, which remained faithful to Spain during the American invasion. They rejected the Masonic Tagalog Katipunan and the revolutionary government led by Aguinaldo. The Cebuanos also

Don Guillermo Gómez Windham

formed their own group, Los Leales Cebuanos, and were responsible for the assassination of revolutionary leader Lieutenant General Pantaleón Villegas y Soldi, also known as León Kilát, in Carcar, Cebu. They accused him of being a Katipunero Mason, a subversive spy, and a recruiter who incited rebellion against Spain. He was fatally stabbed by his aide-de-camp and other Leales.

The assistance provided by the Cebuano and Ylongo populations to Spain put pressure on Aguinaldo to sign the Pacto de Biacnabató truce, agreeing to leave the country and live in exile in Hong Kong. Spain granted him and some of his followers amnesty and monetary compensation, effectively ending the Katipunan's revolution against Spain.

❦

ONLY AFTER SPAIN had signed the Treaty of Paris, relinquishing control of the Philippines to the United States, did the Ylongos and Cebuanos join Aguinaldo in his quest for independence, leading to the establishment of la República Filipina. This newly formed government rejected the Treaty of Paris and refused to acknowledge American sovereignty.

Despite the end of the Spanish-American War with the signing of the Treaty of Paris, the Americans remained determined to subjugate the Philippines and exploit its natural resources, leading to a brutal and one-sided war that caused immense suffering to the Filipino people. However, this dark reality is often omitted or concealed in the teaching of Philippine revolutionary history.

As a result, Filipino students are unable to differentiate between the relatively small-scale, mostly guerrilla revolt against Spain led by the Katipuneros and the full-blown, bloody Philippine-American War, which claimed the lives of millions of innocent Filipinos. The army of la República Filipina only engaged in significant armed conflicts with Spanish military forces in Cavite.

Located in Muelle Loney, the Iloilo Customs House stands near the site where the steamer España, the vessel that transported Rizal from Dapitan, made a brief stopover on its way to Manila.

THE YLONGOS AND Cebuanos initially paid little attention to Rizal's writings against Spain as the Spanish-American War loomed larger in their lives. They saw him as a foreigner who wrote against the Spanish government because of his family's ejectment case filed by the Spanish Dominican Order.

The American colonial government established a new educational system in the Philippines and imposed Rizal as a hero on the Visayans and Mindanaoans. They promoted Rizal and the Katipunan uprising to create animosity toward the Spaniards and divert attention from the war atrocities committed by the Americans during the Philippine-American War.

Today, Rizal's time in Iloilo is largely forgotten, with those who do remember often associating it with the strong-willed Iloilo matriarch who refused to host him in her home. Rizal only gained widespread recognition in Iloilo through the writings of Ylongo hispanistas like the Gómez Windhams, who praised him as a talented Masonic brother who later converted back to Catholicism, as evidenced by his handwritten retraction.

On the left side of the photo is the San José church and convent, facing Rosario Street where the Gómez-Windham mansion (marked with an arrow) is located. To the right of the Gómez-Windham mansion is the Coscuella mansion. The photo was captured a few years after Rizal's visit to the Gómez-Windham mansion.

※

IT WAS DURING the American colonial rule when all the statues and the street named after Rizal in Iloilo City were established. However, as the older, Spanish-speaking Visayans who possessed a deep understanding of how he was deified by the education system created by the Americans pass away, the masses are left with an inadequate comprehension of Rizal. Nowadays, many Filipinos associate him with brand names of daily products, such as the now-defunct zarzaparilla (soft drink), the peso bill that carries his image, or a holiday that bears his name.

The life and legacy of Rizal are undoubtedly significant in Philippine history. Regrettably, many Filipinos only have a vague understanding of him, and his contribution to the country's independence is limited to what they learned in elementary school. This common perception is shaped by the propaganda that surrounded Rizal's execution by the Spanish colonial government, which portrayed the Spaniards as the evil villains who killed the national hero. However, this distorted narrative does a disservice to the Filipino people by preventing them from fully comprehending the complexities of Philippine history.

The Spanish colonization of the Philippines had a significant and positive impact on the country's culture and history. However, when the Americans arrived in the Philippines in 1899, they aimed to pacify the country by demonizing Spain, the colonial ruler they supplanted. This manipulation of Philippine history by foreigners resulted in a built-in bias against the Spanish language among Philippine politicians and education policymakers. This, in turn, has

Above is an old photograph featuring the palatial homes that can be found in the población of Sector de Mestizos or Parián de Molo, a district in Iloilo that José Rizal visited during his brief stay in the city. On the left, you can see the Yusay-Consing residence, which is still considered a landmark in Molo today. Below is the Molo (St. Anne) Roman Catholic Parish Church.

resulted in a lack of understanding of Rizal's works, as most of his brilliant ideas about nationhood were written in Spanish.

Historian Renato Constantino has pointed out that Filipinos have a tendency to venerate Rizal without fully comprehending his ideas. National Artist Nick Joaquín has also remarked that Rizal is a foreigner and a dead foreigner at that. This statement may seem harsh, but it underscores the sad truth that Filipinos are unable to fully understand their national hero. It is a tragedy that Filipinos are the only people who cannot directly access their national hero's works because of the lack of emphasis on the Spanish language.

Despite Senators Claro M. Recto and José P. Laurel's enactment of a law that instituted the teaching of the Rizal course in college, it failed to recognize the importance of the Spanish language in fully understanding Rizal's works. In 1987, the Philippine Constitution abolished the teaching of Spanish in schools and universities, further distancing Filipinos from their national hero.

The legacy of distorted history and cultural incongruence left by the Philippines' former colonial master, the Americans, has had profound and far-reaching consequences. Filipinos have been hindered in their ability to access their cultural heritage and their understanding of their history has been distorted. It is imperative that Filipinos recognize this legacy and work toward a more complete and accurate understanding of their past.

In particular, it is crucial for Filipinos to move beyond the oversimplified portrayal of Rizal as a victim of Spanish oppression and recognize the ways in

National Artist Nick Joaquín   Historian Renato Constantino

During the American colonial era in Iloilo, one of the monuments built was a large statue of José Rizal located in Plaza Libertad. However, some Ylongo political leaders desired to replace it with a statue of General Martín Teófilo Delgado. An important point to consider is that Rizal's recognition among the Ylongos was a result of the efforts of local hispanistas and brother Masons who wrote about him.

which his legacy has been manipulated to demonize Spain. Rizal's ideas were shaped by a unique cultural and historical context, and his multifaceted legacy must be understood in its full complexity.

By understanding the complexities of Philippine history and embracing their cultural heritage, Filipinos can develop a deeper appreciation of their identity and a stronger sense of national pride.

It is time to move beyond the distorted narrative that perpetuates negative stereotypes of Spain and recognize that this skewed portrayal does not fully capture the richness of Philippine history.

Chapter II
The Legendary Teniente Guimó

The memory of Teniente Guimó may have faded over time, as the newer generation of Ylongos are presumably better educated and have more important things to focus on than the fantastic tales of sorcery attributed to this feared figure. Yet, his name remains well-known, and the mere mention of his notoriety as a sorcerer (asuang) still sends shivers down people's spines. While there are several exciting stories about him in Philippine folklore, one in particular stands out: that of a young public schoolteacher who was invited to stay overnight at his daughter's house, only to discover that she would be killed if she didn't run for her life.

Until recently, the name Teniente Guimó was associated with bad news, particularly for tourism on Panay Island. Just the mention of his name was enough to scare away visitors. It was rumored that many of his descendants, believed to be practicing witchcraft (inasuañgon), still lived in Capiz. But who was the real Teniente Guimó, and why did his name become legendary to the point where it still triggers a mixed bag of emotions, such as enchantment and trepidation, even among today's supposedly sophisticated Ylongos?

From Ylongos born in the mid-1930s who were curious enough to ask their elders about Teniente Guimó, a clearer picture emerges of this strategic mythical sorcerer, who allegedly used his supernatural powers to fight against foreign invaders. People called him "Teniente" because he was a teniente del barrio or village chief. Guimó is clearly a nickname derived from Guillermo (William).

In this author's childhood, we had a nanny from Calinog named Imang, a moniker for Guillerma. Although Imang never went to school, she was a font of knowledge in oral traditions, including *Ang Maragtas sang Panay*, composos, hurubatons, and refranes in old Kinaray-a Ylongo as well as in modern Hiligaynon. She was also well-versed in the old Ylongo corridos like *Don Juan Tiñoso* and several cuentos, which center around three princesses who meet and fall in love with three princes in an adventure of "Moros y Cristianos" and live happily ever after. Imang personally knew Teniente Guimó's family and claimed that he was a real sorcerer.

Imang revealed that Teniente Guimó's last name was Guillerán. Using the old Spanish empadronamiento, we can narrow down the list of towns his family came from. The Spaniards created a catalog of Spanish surnames in alphabetical order for Filipino natives to use. The catalog, entitled *Catálogo Alfabético de Apellidos*, was published in 1849 and consisted of one hundred forty-one pages of Spanish and native surnames. Spanish Governor-General Narciso Claveria y Zaldúa, along with Domingo Abella, created the catalog following a decree Claveria issued in November 1849 to eliminate confusion that arose from colonial subjects not having a last name. When the catalog reached local government units, the gobernadorcillos assigned each town a number of pages from the catalog from which their constituents could choose a surname. For the sake of convenience and efficiency, they matched the first letter of the town's name with the first letter of the surnames listed on the pages of the catalog. Therefore, Guillerán could be from either Guimbal or nearby Guimarás Island.

※

DINGLE, A TOWN with a predominantly native population, had seven families of Spanish descent, including the Dayots, Monteros, Hernándezes, Gaviras, Guilleráns, and Dators. In addition, the barrios of Tabugón and Santa Rufina were home to three other prominent Spanish families: the Roceses, Gayosos, and Riveras. Teniente Guimó was a member of the Hernández Gavira-Guillerán clans, which originated from a union between a Guillerán from Guimarás and a Hernández Gavira maiden. Their son, Eugenio, married an indianeta from Laglag named Dumalogdog, and their child, Guillermo, was later known as Teniente Guimó.

During his teenage years, Guillermo Guillerán y Dumalogdog joined the Batallón de Voluntarios Ylongos, which was formed by the Ylongos themselves to assist the Spanish regular army in defending the Philippines.

The Ylongos were concerned about an impending U.S. invasion due to anti-Spanish sentiments in the American press, which accused Spain of oppressing Cuba. It was not long before the U.S. formally declared war, and it became apparent to everyone that the U.S. was attempting to seize Spain's overseas possessions, including Cuba, Puerto Rico, Guam, and the Philippines. President William McKinley later

Following the signing of the Treaty of Paris on December 10, 1898 that marked the end of the Spanish-American War, the Spanish authorities days later symbolically transferred the Philippines to General Martín Teófilo Delgado. The Voluntarios, who had organized themselves to help the Spanish regular army defend the Philippines against the anticipated U.S. invasion, stand in formation at Plaza Alfonso XII to witness this historic event.

referred to the decision to colonize the Philippines as America's "Manifest Destiny."

※

GENERAL MARTÍN TEÓFILO Delgado y Bermejo, a Spanish mestizo, was chosen to lead the battalion of Ylongo military men and officers like Venancio Concepción and General Adriano Hernández of Dingle. When news of the Treaty of Paris between Spain and the United States reached Iloilo, the Spanish civil authorities and military forces turned over the government to the Voluntarios under Delgado and left for Zamboanga.

General Martín Teófilo Delgado

Later on, the Voluntarios joined the República Filipina of Aguinaldo, which was at war with the invading Americans who had taken over Manila and its surrounding provinces.

After Manila was subdued, the Americans sent gunboats headed by the *USS Petrel* to Iloilo. However, the Voluntarios, now part of the Aguinaldo forces, did not allow the American invaders under General Marcus P. Miller to land in Iloilo. This resistance infuriated the Americans, who then ordered the *USS Petrel* and the *USS Baltimore* to shell the city of Iloilo and the municipality of Jaro. Under the cover of this indiscriminate bombardment, the American forces could finally land. Despite the Voluntarios' valiant efforts, the American occupation of Iloilo City, Jaro, and other towns was only delayed, not prevented.

The Americans used military force, diplomacy, and psychological warfare to achieve their goals, and the Ylongo defenses eventually crumbled before the American onslaught. While most of the Voluntarios were forced to capitulate due to exhaustion and lack of arms and ammunition, Teniente Guimó refused to surrender. He found a suitable mountain redoubt in Mount Bulabog-Putian near Dueñas, where the thick jungles in the nearby barrios of Banug, Tabugón, Tinocuan, and Santa Rufina provided extra protection.

In Cebu, the Cebuano Leales were also preparing to confront the Americans, led by General Arcadio Maxilom y Molero, who had united with President Aguinaldo against the invaders. However, to avoid bloodshed, Father (later Bishop) Juan Bautista Gorordo y Perfecto negotiated a peaceful surrender of the city aboard the *USS Petrel*.

As the American occupation advanced in the provinces of Iloilo, Antique, and Capiz, they also organized public elementary schools in every barrio. The spread of these schools weakened Ylongo resistance, leading to the surrender of most of the Voluntarios turned insurrectos and revolucionarios. However, Teniente Guimó remained determined to fight and held out in his mountain redoubt near Dueñas.

※

AMID THE TUMULT of war, Teniente Guimó managed to secretly raise a family in a sprawling stone house that had been passed down from his parents in Dingle. His daughter Saturnina, who ran a small carindería, resided with him in the ancestral home. Meanwhile, in Dueñas, he owned another stone house which was run by his wife Florencia and adult son Alfonso. Alfonso quietly lived there with his wife and children who worked as cooks for weddings, baptisms, and town fiestas. Despite efforts made by the Constabulary and the town police, Teniente Guimó remained elusive and successfully avoided capture. The safety of Guimó and his family remained unscathed, thanks to some form of sorcery that defied the efforts of the American military authorities to locate him. The primary classes

The legend of Teniente Guimó lives on in the public consciousness, as evidenced by movies that have been made about him.

Don Esteban Lanza, brother of the slain Rafael Lanza.

were also disturbed by the mysterious disappearances of several female public schoolteachers, which only added to the mystery surrounding Teniente Guimó and his family.

Teniente Guimó had a keen sense of the American-organized public school system's ulterior motives. He believed it was an attempt to indoctrinate school-age children into accepting the economic colonialism that the Americans were beginning to impose on the country. However, the American pacification campaign managed to quell any resistance to their rule.

The 1940s rolled around, and the bloody Japanese invasion overwhelmed all of Panay Island, the rest of the Visayas, and eventually Mindanao. During the four-year Japanese occupation of Iloilo, Teniente Guimó's name became entangled in a rather interesting and unfortunate incident involving the assassination of Rafael Lanza, the Spanish-Filipino husband of Encarnación Miller, a daughter of an American military officer who was part of the American invasion.

Rafael's father, the famous Iloilo writer Don Esteban Lanza, harshly criticized the American administration for corruption in his widely-read newspaper columns in *El Porvenir de Visayas* and other Iloilo dailies like *El Adalid* and *El Heraldo*. His satirical essays later became a book in two volumes entitled *Crónicas Visayas*. The USAFFE (United States Army Forces Far East) guerrilla unit responsible for the assassination mistook Rafael for his father, Don Esteban.

This incident left Teniente Guimó deeply distraught, as he was an ardent follower of Don Esteban's anti-American writings under the pseudonym "Isla de Panay." He sought vengeance for Rafael's death by hunting down the families of the soldiers responsible for his murder. Using various forms of sorcery that terrified many people, he killed their mothers, wives, daughters, sisters, and other family members across Panay. Despite efforts made by the guilty murderers to locate Teniente Guimó, he remained elusive, and most of them later met their demise in several encounters with the Japanese army.

After the Japanese-American War ended, many clamored to make Teniente Guimó a hero of Iloilo for resisting American colonization and fighting the Japanese through sorcery, such as usug, halit, and durá. Don Vicente Ybiernas, a prominent Iloilo elder, even suggested that the statue of José Rizal in Plaza Liber-

The gunboat USS Petrel is shown stationed at Hong Kong harbor, April 15, 1898, It was one of the vessels that, along with the cruiser USS Baltimore, participated in the bombardment of Iloilo City on February 11, 1899. This attack paved the way for the U.S. First Separate Brigade led by Brigadier General Marcus P. Miller to disembark and take control of the area.

tad be replaced with one of Teniente Guimó in his Voluntario uniform. However, the government authorities ignored his proposal and similar recommendations. Nevertheless, the name of Teniente Guimó remains significant and continues to be part of the Ylongo-Panayanon identity.

Chapter III
Teniente Guimó's Dueñas Forebears

The city and the province of Iloilo are progressing economically thanks to modern political leadership, but there is also a strong desire among the people to preserve the Ylongo culture, history, and language. As other Panay provinces follow in Iloilo's footsteps, there is a growing interest in Ylongo vernacular folklore, particularly the Teniente Guimó phenomenon.

Teniente Guimó's mother belonged to the Domalogdog family, which is traceable to the towns of Dingle and Dueñas under the Spanish empadronamiento system. Dueñas was formerly known as "Laglag" when it was just a distant barrio of Dingle. Even today, some areas in Dueñas are not easily accessible. A neighboring town is Pototan, where Teresa Magbanua, a schoolteacher, fought against the American invaders.

During our adolescence, we knew a Domalogdog residing in Tinocuan, a small barrio between Dingle and Dueñas. This man was a hardworking and frugal aparcero who managed sugarcane fields for the author's hacendero grandfather, José Rivera. The sugarcane was harvested, trucked to Central Azucarera de Dumalág (which was owned by the Ford-Garcia family), and refined into sugar. A small portion of the harvest was also processed into brown sugar by Domalogdog at his own muscovado mill.

However, one day, he disappeared without a trace, leaving everyone in the barrio surprised and frightened. The women in the barrio even exclaimed "Asuang!" with fear written all over their faces, and tightened their patadiongs around their waists while straightening their transparent quimonas covering their breasts.

The aparcero who disappeared was rumored to be a descendant of one of the ten Bornean datus who arrived in Panay with Datu Puti. This datu was known as Domalogdog and was believed to possess magical powers and be an asuang, or sorcerer. The women in the community used this historical context to explain why Teniente Guimó also became a sorcerer; it was believed that he inherited the magical genes and powers of his ancestor. Teniente Guimó's mother was said to be a descendant of an ancient pre-Hispanic family that traced its lineage to Datu Domalogdog. It is difficult to depict Teniente Guimó's appearance without imagining the native features of his Domalogdog lineage mixed with the Andalusian Spanish characteristics of his Guillerán ancestry.

Teniente Guimó was a man of many talents, not only did he have a medical background as a physician, but he was also a skilled warrior. It is believed that he completed his medical studies at the University of Santo Tomás with the help of

General Ananías Diokno and his military expeditionary force from Luzon were perceived as invaders by the Ylongos, as witnessed by some of their members.

the Guillerán-Hernández-Gavira fortunes, a little-known tidbit that was recounted by Don Benito Roces and his sister, María Luz Roces. Interestingly, María Luz' daughter, Judy Jalbuena Syjuco, is the mother of the award-winning novelist Miguel Syjuco.

After completing his medical training, Teniente Guimó returned to Dingle and enlisted as a Voluntario to defend Spain against an impending American invasion. Along with many others from Dingle and Dueñas, he was determined to protect his country from the incoming threat. However, despite their best efforts, the Spaniards were eventually forced to withdraw from Iloilo with the signing of the Treaty of Paris. Teniente Guimó then joined the Aguinaldo army to fight against the invading American forces led by General Miller.

Unfortunately, the resistance was no match for the superior arms of the American forces, and it was only a matter of time before all resistance ended. In 1901, General Ananías Diokno, who headed a military expeditionary force sent from Luzon by Aguinaldo to bring Iloilo under the control and sovereignty of the latter's politico-military government, was wounded in a skirmish and captured.

Despite the efforts of Aguinaldo to consolidate his power throughout the country, his revolutionary government against Spain failed to gain recognition from many ethnic groups, including the Ylongos and other Visayans, as well as the Mindanaoans under the Provisional Revolutionary Government of the Visayas and Mindanao.

In Panay, Diokno's military contingent was considered an invading Tagalog force and was met with hostility by the residents. The Ylongos formed their own government to manage their affairs and resist the American invasion. General

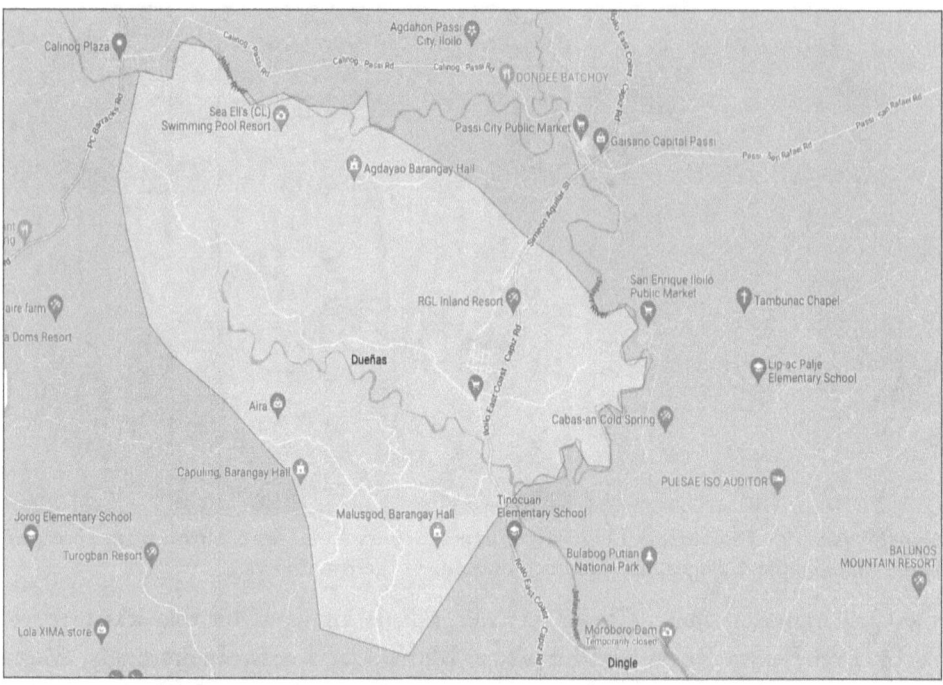

A map of Dueñas town and surrounding areas showing the general vicinity where Teniente Guimó operated as a guerrilla warrior against the American military forces.

Delgado proclaimed this government during the "Cry of Santa Bárbara" in Iloilo on November 17, 1898. Shortly after, it was replaced by a federal government, which led the fight against the American invasion.

Throughout this tumultuous time, Teniente Guimó remained steadfast in his commitment to defending his country, despite the odds against him. His medical background and expertise were undoubtedly valuable assets during the conflict, but it was his determination and bravery that truly set him apart. The legacy of Teniente Guimó lives on as a reminder of the courage and resilience of the Filipino people in the face of adversity.

※

TENIENTE GUIMÓ WAS not willing to surrender to the Americans even after other Ylongo military leaders had been captured or neutralized by the new colonial rulers. He knew that he had to fight until the last breath and did not want his daughter to be caught in the crossfire, so he left her behind to maintain their ancestral balay nga bato in Dingle. He took refuge in the Puti-an Bulabog mountains and became an asuang or sorcerer to fight against the American invaders.

As a student in Manila, Teniente Guimó had joined the Masons and learned the black arts, which he used to acquire mystical powers of the Cabaliststs. These powers strengthened his genetic predisposition not only as a sorcerer but as a cannibal. In his hideout, he preyed upon public elementary schoolteachers, whom he considered to be allies of the American invaders who were establishing schools throughout Panay to win the hearts and minds of the people through education skewed toward accepting the American colonial regime.

Teniente Guimó captured and turned the teachers into deer and hogs for food, building an impregnable stronghold in the enchanted caves of Puti-an, which merited a mention in Félix Laureano's *Recuerdos de Filipinas*. He knew that the Americans were training the teachers to teach English to wean away young Filipinos from the national cause of freedom. As word of his unconventional resistance spread far and wide, other Ylongo patriots who reportedly possessed anito powers linked arms with him in the struggle.

Among those who joined him was the mythical Labao Dungon, who became a super anito warrior. However, how their struggle ended remains unknown. Legend has it that they are still hiding somewhere in the sacred Madia-as mountain and will return someday to free Iloilo from American colonialism.

Another iteration of the speculations swirling around the Teniente Guimó legend claims that he derived his mystical powers from Michael the Archangel. The Chief Prince of the Heavenly came down from heaven, cured him of his cannibalistic tendencies, and sanctified him from the grip of the black arts, leaving him with supernatural powers to fight for his Ylongo people until they achieve true liberty. This version of the legend adds a spiritual dimension to Teniente Guimó's character, suggesting that he had a divine mission to defend his people against the American invaders.

Guillermo Gómez Rivera's novel features Teniente Guimó, a supernatural figure at the center of its plot, as depicted on the cover.

Chapter IV
THE NEED FOR AN INDEPENDENT HISTORY

The city of Iloilo, once a bulwark of the Philippines' struggle against the United States in the Philippine-American War at the turn of the twentieth century, has lost much of its historical significance to its own people. Today, many Ylongos are unaware of their city's rich history, let alone the role it played in the country's struggle for independence.

One of the reasons for this lack of awareness can be traced back to the American colonial period, when the country's present education system was first developed. The Americans aimed to mold young Filipinos into welcoming them as "saviors" who liberated the country from the "evil" Spaniards. As a result, the education system became a tool for pacification, perpetuating a distorted narrative that favored American imperialism and demonized Spanish colonialism.

Over the years, the education system was taken over by bureaucrats who were heavily influenced by the Katipunan culture, imposing their brand of colonialism on the rest of the nation. This led to a Tagalog-centric curriculum, especially in history, where Tagalog Abakada puristas and Katipunan cultists advanced their agenda. Americanized historians like Teodoro A. Agoncillo were instrumental in spreading this falsified version of history.

This one-sided approach to education has resulted in a loss of cultural heritage and a distorted understanding of Philippine history. Many Ylongos today are unable to appreciate the significance of their city in the context of the Philippine Revolution against Spain. The erasure of their city's independent history is a tragedy, one that has long-lasting effects on their cultural identity.

It is essential to recognize the role that the American colonial period played in shaping the education system and how it perpetuated a distorted narrative of Philippine history. It is also crucial to acknowledge the importance of preserving local histories and cultures, especially in cities like Iloilo, where the struggle for independence played a vital role in shaping its identity.

Efforts should be made to provide a balanced and accurate account of Philippine history, one that reflects the complexities and diversity of the country's cultural heritage. Only then can we truly appreciate the struggles and sacrifices of our forebears and gain a better understanding of ourselves as a nation.

Agoncillo, a prominent historian, is known for his strict adherence to the Tagalog Abakada-Balarila purista ideology, which was evident in his published article that insisted on spelling "Florante" as "Plorante." This stance revealed his true colors as a purist who believed in upholding the strictest rules of the Tagalog language.

However, Agoncillo's purist beliefs extended beyond language and into the realm of history, where he pushed the fabricated idea that all Filipinos were united under the Katipunan in the fight against Spain. This is a gross oversimplification of history and ignores the fact that many non-Tagalog ethnic groups, such as the Ylongos and other Visayans, had their own ideas for bringing about reforms without resorting to revolution.

Rudymar "Dinggol" Divinagracia Araneta

In reality, the Visayans never joined the Tagalog Katipunan of Masons under Andrés Bonifacio, José Rizal, and Emilio Aguinaldo to fight against what was called Spanish colonialism. The limited nature of the revolution can also be seen in the flag sewn in Taal town by Marcela Agoncillo, which contained eight sun rays representing only the eight Tagalog provinces that revolted against Spain. This exclusion of the provinces outside of Luzon, such as those in the Visayas, particularly Iloilo and Cebu, is a testament to the fact that they were never part of the revolution started by the Katipunan.

In sum, Agoncillo's purist beliefs, while admirable in the eyes of his followers, led him to overlook the complex and diverse nature of Philippine history, and to oversimplify the revolution against Spanish colonialism.

The way history is taught in the Philippines is often riddled with biases, particularly the Tagalog-centric perspective that seeks to glorify the Abakada Katipunan revolution. However, this version of history conveniently neglects to acknowledge the bravery and sacrifices made by the Ylongo Voluntarios and the Cebuano Leales who fought on the side of Spain.

The Tagalog puristas fail to mention that volunteer groups were formed by Tagalogs, Bicolanos, Pampangos, and Ilocanos in support of Spain. Unfortunately, their slanted version of history has been drilled into the minds of non-Tagalog schoolchildren for over a century, turning the Tagalog puristas into cultural colonizers of Visayans and other non-Tagalog groups.

The school curriculum is crafted by these Tagalog-centric colonizers from imperial Manila, perpetuating a false narrative concerning history and language. This has led many new generations of Ylongos to believe that their forebears supported the Tagalog Katipuneros under the leadership of Bonifacio, Rizal, and Aguinaldo.

In fact, the Ylongos formed the Batallón Ylongo de Voluntarios and the Cebuanos organized the Batallones de Cebuanos Leales to fight for their own causes. Historian and researcher Rudymar "Dinggol" Araneta Divinagracia even revealed the existence of an Estado Federal de Visayas presided over by Ylongo Raymundo Melliza, which later became a part of the República de Filipinas of Aguinaldo. The Ylongos shaped their independent history without the dictates of the Katipunan, but they were also pragmatists and realists, ultimately joining forces with Aguinaldo to fight against the superior American forces.

It is crucial to teach schoolchildren the truth about history and acknowledge the contributions of all ethnic groups in shaping the nation's identity. We must move past the biases of the past and embrace a more inclusive and accurate understanding of our history.

❧

THE YLONGOS HAVE have a rich pre-Hispanic oral history and traditions, which have been passed down from one generation to the next by word of mouth. These stories include the *Maragtas sang Panay*, *Código de Calanti-ao*, *Código de Sumacuel*, *Romance Between Sumacuel and Alayon-Capinangan*, *Diez Datos de Borneo*, *Barter of Panay*, *Madia-as Confederation*, and many others.

Despite their long-standing existence and widespread transmission, some historians like William Henry Scott have labeled these oral traditions as "hoaxes." This dismissal has angered the Ylongos, who see the evidence of their culture and history in these stories. It seems that these historians are too quick to ignore any evidence that does not support their theory that the *Maragtas* is a "myth" solely because it "has no written documents."

In response, Ylongo scholars like Divinagracia have questioned why these mostly Manila-based historians are so fixated on written documents when oral traditions have been a recognized method of transmitting history and culture for centuries. The fact that these stories were passed down orally should not be a reason to discredit them.

This dismissal of Ylongo pre-Hispanic history is highly unfair and unjustified, especially when compared to the myth of Lapu-lapu killing Magellan in hand-to-hand combat. This myth has been heavily promoted by some historians, despite the lack of any written evidence to support it. The only documentation about the Battle of Mactan comes from Antonio Pigafetta, the chronicler of Magellan's voyage that reached the Philippines in 1521. It clearly belies the myth about Magellan's death in the hands of Lapu-lapu.

Despite this, the myth has been taken as dogma for more than a century, while the rich oral history of the Ylongos has been dismissed as mere fantasy. It is time to reevaluate how we view and study history and recognize the value of different methods of transmitting information.

Interestingly, nowhere in Pigafetta's account does it say that Lapu-lapu personally killed Magellan:

> Recognizing the captain [Magellan], so many turned upon him that they knocked his helmet off his head twice, but he always stood firmly like a good knight, together with some others. Thus did we fight for more than one hour, refusing to retire farther.
>
> One of them wounded him on the left leg with a large cutlass, which resembles a scimitar, only being larger. That caused the captain to fall face downward, when

General Martín Teófilo Delgado and his troops, consisting of thirty officers and one hundred forty soldiers, march toward Brigadier General Edmund Rice, the U.S. military governor of Panay, to surrender on February 2, 1901.

immediately they rushed upon him with iron and bamboo spears and with their cutlasses, until they killed our mirror, our light, our comfort, and our true guide.

※

THE MARAGTAS WAS meticulously documented in the 1850s by Fray Tomás Santarén, a Spanish Augustinian friar who had a deep respect for the Ylongo oral traditions. His dedication allowed him to transcribe these tales and translate them into Spanish, preserving the rich and colorful heritage of the Ylongo people. His work proved invaluable to later generations of Ylongo Ilustrados, including the King of Ylongo Poetry, Delfín Gumbán, and Flavio Zaragoza Cano, both of whom used Fray Santarén's translations as a source of inspiration for their own literary works.

However, some historians, such as Henry Scott, have been casting doubt on the authenticity of the Ylongo oral traditions, contributing to the marginalization of the Ylongos in Philippine history. This pattern was established by American colonizers and Tagalog Abakada puristas such as Lope K. Santos and Teodoro A. Agoncillo, who have contributed to the official exclusion of the Ylongo pre-Hispanic *Maragtas*, leading to a revision of Philippine history that borders on absurdity.

Agoncillo once claimed that history must be written from the Filipino point of view, but this statement is hypocritical at best. The *truth* must be the *only* valid point of view in any historical account. Agoncillo himself even admitted that defining what it means to be Filipino is challenging, if not impossible. However, as a historian, it was his duty to provide clarity on this matter. He could have consulted with *Webster's Dictionary,* which defines a Filipino as "a member of a Christianized Malayan tribe (or people) as distinguished from the wild tribes and the Mohammedan Moors."

Unfortunately, authors like Agoncillo, who is regarded as a "state historian," have played an outsized role in shaping our understanding of Philippine history. As a result, many Filipinos today are woefully ignorant of their heritage, and some even despise it. It is time to re-evaluate the way history is written and taught in the Philippines, with a renewed emphasis on accuracy and inclusivity.

※

AS PROUD YLONGOS AND Filipinos, we must raise concerns about the neocolonization of our children through education by a small group of Americanized Tagalog puristas from Manila. These puristas, blindly following the damaging American

THE INDEPENDENT HISTORY OF YLONGO AND CEBUANO VISAYANS

"Boxer Codex," a Spanish manuscript created in the Philippines dating back to 1590, showcases portraits of Visayan noble pairs in the late sixteenth century.

agenda of a totalitarian history, are using non-Tagalog tax money to impose cultural colonialism upon non-Tagalogs, including the Ylongo Visayans. They are pushing a revisionist version of our national history with inaccuracies and even plain inventions to mislead our youth.

To truly recover our past, Ylongos must recall their undiluted history, particularly during the *Maragtas*, Leales Voluntarios for Spain of 1898, and the establishment of the Estado Federal de Visayas. These pivotal historical events instilled pride in every Ylongo and Cebuano, and must be brought to the forefront as they represent the independent spirit of the Ylongos during a time when the United States launched a war of territorial aggression against Spain for economic greed.

Unfortunately, the Tagalog Abakada puristas are entrenched in our educational system, aiming to mislead our schoolchildren with false narratives and conclusions. They even meddle with our native languages, introducing absurd Balarila words like salumpuwit and sugnay at parirala, and replacing native Filipino sounds like the consonant "F" with "P" in critical proper nouns such as Filipinas and Filipino.

We must take action to stop this cultural oppression and preserve our true history and heritage.

CHAPTER V
REAL BENEVOLENCE: SPANISH CITIZENSHIP

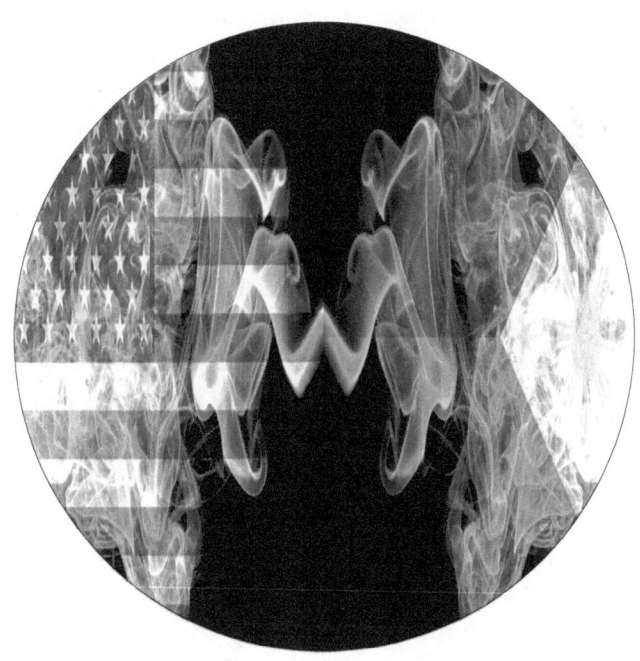

The American policy of "benevolent assimilation" in the colonization of the Philippines has long been considered a sham. The United States had never intended to grant the Philippines statehood in the American union, and this was made clear by the fact that Filipinos were never granted U.S. citizenship, with the exception of those who immigrated to the United States and eventually became citizens. Instead, it appears that overt racism was the true reason behind this exclusion.

In contrast, Spain, as a Catholic country, showed genuine benevolence toward the indigenous people of the Philippines. Spain bestowed citizenship upon Filipinos who accepted the Spanish King as their "natural sovereign (monarch)." From the beginning of the Spanish colonization of the Philippines in 1565, Philip II made it clear that he wanted the Filipinos to know God in order to develop and progress individually. To this end, he decreed that they be taught catechism at the expense of the Spanish Crown. The friars initially accomplished this charge by turning their convents into schools, instructing native children on religion and the three Rs: reading, writing, and arithmetic, and later establishing proper schools.

The Spanish focus on teaching the basics of civilized life extended far beyond religious instruction. The goal was to instill in the Filipinos a more advanced way of life as Christians. This meant teaching them everything from better agricultural techniques to support their families, to reading and writing in Spanish, to appreciating the arts and sciences, to starting businesses and becoming self-sufficient. In essence, the Spanish frailes acted as mentors, guiding the Filipinos toward a more cultured and civilized way of life.

The Spanish influence on the Filipino way of life was so profound that a life cycle was established that began at birth and continued through death. From baptism to marriage and even death, the Filipino way of life was intertwined with Catholicism and Spanish culture. This fundamental "Spanishness" of the Filipinos was a product of the benevolent assimilation practiced by the Spanish colonial administration.

However, with the arrival of the American colonialists, everything changed. Instead of building upon the foundations laid by the Spaniards, the Americans foisted their language, pop culture, and foreign debt onto the Philippines. This foreign influence has had a disastrous effect on the country and its people. Corruption has become endemic, with crooked politicians enriching themselves by robbing the national coffers. The national budget is bloated with pork barrel spending,

This painting shows a significant moment in the history of the Spanish Cortes in Cadíz as they convened to draft the groundbreaking Spanish Constitution of 1812. The constitution was a milestone as it granted Spanish citizenship to Filipinos and elevated the Philippines from a mere overseas possession to a province of the Kingdom of Spain. Ventura de los Reyes, the Philippines' sole delegate, played a vital role in the deliberations.

and government projects are mired in financial scandals due to the purchase of substandard and overpriced equipment.

Even during the Covid-19 pandemic, wayward officials allegedly took advantage of the situation by purchasing overpriced life-saving health and hospital equipment. This greed has resulted in the impoverishment of most Filipinos, dooming them to a hopeless existence marked by terrible suffering, hunger, poverty, and ignorance.

While corruption existed during the Spanish administration, it was not as damaging to the Filipinos as the kind of monstrous corruption that we see today. The legacy of the American colonization of the Philippines has been a poisonous one. Instead of building upon the foundations laid by the Spaniards, the Americans have left the country and its people in a state of chaos, with little hope for a brighter future. It is a stark reminder of the dangers of imperialism and colonization, and a warning to future generations to be wary of foreign influences that seek to exploit and control their way of life.

DURING THE AMERICAN colonial period in the Philippines, a fervent movement for statehood emerged, driven by the aspirations of Benito Legarda, Trinidad Pardo de Tavera, and Gregorio S. Araneta, all esteemed Filipinos hailing from old, established families of Spanish and chino cristiano descent. The Federalist Party, under which these illustrious figures banded together, made statehood a cornerstone of their platform.

However, this noble goal was met with an insidious force lurking within the American government and society: racism. Behind the Americans' mask of benevolence lay a core of prejudice, a fact that these passionate statehood advocates failed to recognize. Foremost among these bigots was Elihu Root, a high-ranking official and instrumental figure in shaping colonial policy in the Philippines during the presidencies of William McKinley and Theodore Roosevelt.

As Julian Go expounds in a scathing article on racism and colonialism in the journal *Qualitative Sociology*, Root deemed Filipinos as "children" who were "locked in a rudimentary state of political development," thus rendering them unfit for modern self-government. Root further asserted that granting the Philippines independence would prove a "fatal gift" to its people.

Such racist views were rampant in the era, as evidenced by the infamous diatribe of Hubert Howe Bancroft, a Western United States historian who espoused his contempt for people of color:

> Have we not already absorbed enough of the base blood of Europe and the black blood of Africa? Now we are bringing upon ourselves a horde of that hybrid population found in the Spanish colonies, made up of endless inter-mixtures of Indians (Indios), Negroes and Spaniards, together with the Kanakas (Indios) of Hawaii and the Mongolians (Chinese) of the Asiatic Isles, with all their still lower and more degrading inter-mixtures.

Howe's unabashed xenophobia toward Asians was evident in his book, *History of California*, which was published in 1890.

> These people were true, in every sense, aliens. The color of their skins, the repulsiveness of their features, their undersize figure, their incomprehensible language, strange customs, and heathen religion...conspired to set them apart.

•

The imperialists' opposition to Philippine statehood was but a manifestation of this reprehensible mindset, which the enlightened and visionary leaders of the time fought to overcome.

On the opposite end of the spectrum, the Catholic Spaniards and former colonial masters of the Philippines held a different perspective and embraced the mestizaje (mestizo) culture. Unlike their American counterparts, they had no qualms about intermarrying with the native population, having been exposed for generations to different cultures that coexisted and cohabited harmoniously in their own kingdom. They even took pride in the fact that the sixteenth-century city of Toledo was a melting pot of three cultures: Jewish, Christian, and Muslim.

This liberal attitude had its roots in the Age of Exploration when Queen Isabel instructed the conquistadores in the New World to promote mixed marriages with the indigenous people. As early as 1503, she explained the rationale for this policy to the governor of the Indies (Hispaniola), Nicolás de Ovando, stating that it was "legitimate and recommended because the Indians are free vassals of the Spanish Crown." In terms of mixed marriages, this progressive policy was five hundred years ahead of the United States, where interracial marriage was legalized only in 1967 after the Supreme Court declared antimiscegenation laws in some states unconstitutional.

Although the Civil Rights Movement led by Martin Luther King Jr. resulted in the passage of the Civil Rights Act in 1964, which outlawed discrimination on the basis of sex, race, creed, or national origin, racial crimes against Blacks, Asians, and Hispanics continue to plague American society. Despite the progress made in the fight for racial equality and justice, some ignorant Americans persist in clinging to their racist beliefs, leading to dire consequences. One of the most heinous recent cases was the death of George Floyd, who died while in police custody, sparking demands to defund the police. The chilling phrase that Floyd uttered as he implored the police has become synonymous with the plea for racial equality and justice: "I can't breathe."

In the Philippines, the rise of the Tagalog Abakada purista culture has fueled Hispanophobia and Sinophobia among many "modern Pinoys." Sadly, this intolerance extends even to the correct use and spelling of Spanish words that have already become part of Tagalog and other major native languages. An excellent example of this is their insistence on replacing F with P in Filipinas and Filipino, simply because F is Spanish ("kasi, ang F ay Kastila").

CHAPTER VI
WHY VISAYANS SIDED WITH SPAIN

Undoubtedly, Spain has had a significant influence on all aspects of Filipino society over the centuries. However, a small faction of Tagalog supremacists and Abakada purists, who have embraced Americanization, vigorously refute the constructive outcomes of Spain's colonization of the Philippines. This immature and myopic viewpoint can be attributed to the initial American occupiers who came to the country in 1899. These early Protestant interlopers showed a high degree of sectarian intolerance, and their modern-day followers are just as guilty of ignorance when it comes to understanding our country's true history. They are oblivious to the greatness of our Spanish heritage, which was deeply rooted in the successful Catholization of the country. The friars played a crucial role in achieving King Philip II's edict that Spanish conquest of new lands must go hand in hand with evangelization.

The Abakada Katipunan partisans, on the other hand, were proponents of a neocolonial policy that created a society full of inequities, where Filipinos were treated as commodities and a cheap source of labor. These same politicians continue to exploit Filipinos during elections, and their corruption is a deeply ingrained social problem that even the present Americanized Catholic clergy struggles to cope with. The loss of our Spanish heritage and language has weakened the once-strong bond between the clergy and the Spanish-speaking Catholic lay leaders.

It is time for us as a people to reclaim our Spanish heritage, with its Hispanized Catholic culture, in order to free ourselves from the suffocating Abakada Katipunan ideology and culture that breeds corruption. Unfortunately, Catholicism is losing its influence over the population, with some saying it is becoming a minority religion. Nonetheless, the rich legacy of Spain in our country is something that we must embrace and celebrate. Only then can we truly appreciate the many gifts that Spain has bestowed upon us, and move forward as a unified and proud nation.

※

THE VISAYANS OF the 1890s, particularly the Ylongos, were fiercely loyal to Spain due to the numerous economic and cultural benefits they had reaped from the Spanish conquistadores. Their loyalty was rooted in their gratitude for the advancements that had been introduced to them by the Spaniards, which had catapulted them to new heights of prosperity.

The splendor of the Galleon Trade is exemplified by an image of a Spanish galleon found in the "Boxer Codex," an ageless artifact dating back to the late sixteenth century.

The Spanish missionaries brought modern farming tools, such as the plow and the carabao, from Spain and Vietnam, which proved to be a game-changer for the ancient subsistence farmers who had been reliant on slash-and-burn techniques for generations. These new tools led to improved harvests, allowing the kaingeros to transition into successful farmers, or agricultores, using European agricultural techniques. Over time, they became wealthy rice and sugar farmers, or arroceros and hacenderos, and owners of haciendas-centrales-azucarreras.

With prosperity came new industries, such as the agsadores of rice, corn, coffee, cacao-chocolate, wine, fruit, and vegetable farms. The Galleon Trade between Acapulco and Manila from 1565 to 1815 allowed for the exchange of goods and new ideas, bringing the continents of Asia, Europe, and the Americas closer together. The Bicolano manufacturers of abaca hemp and rope became famous worldwide, while the Spaniards introduced tobacco farming to the Ilocos region, creating an industry that continues to provide income and employment to thousands of people.

The Spanish colonial administration distributed vast tracts of land in Panay, Negros, and Cebu to many indio principalía families, chino cristiano business families, and Spanish-Filipino families who, in just a few generations, became sugar barons. They employed laborers and rice and corn producers who, in turn, generated jobs by enlisting aparceros. Food manufacturing companies were established, employing the native masses. The system wasn't perfect, but it provided economic sustenance to the vast majority of the population and put the country on the path to progress, as depicted in Juan Luna's masterpiece, *España y Filipinas*, where Spain is a mother guiding her daughter, Filipinas, toward a better future.

The Spanish frailes also left their mark, building towns and cities and connecting them with a network of roads and bridges. The Recollects left an impressive architectural legacy in Negros Occidental, with their beautiful churches and other buildings, while the Augustinians undertook similar extraordinary construction projects in Panay. Their evangelical, educational, communal, and social work cannot be underestimated, and their names are remembered in many Iloilo and Negros churches and municipal halls, attesting to their immense contributions to Filipino society.

In addition to the numerous infrastructures and social services that were made available to the locals, the Spanish Crown also granted Spanish citizenship to the chinos cristianos and the Spanish Creole families. These individuals were listed as sujetos del Rey de España or subjects of the King of Spain, and they took great pride in speaking the Spanish language. It is worth noting that when Spain was faced with the threat of war from the United States, the chinos cristianos and Spanish Creole families in Iloilo and Cebu banded together and formed battalions to defend Spain and its overseas territories. Their unwavering support for Spain demonstrated the deep loyalty and gratitude they had for the benefits and privileges they had received under Spanish rule.

In brief, the Visayans' loyalty to Spain was well-founded, as the Spanish conquistadores had brought real economic and cultural benefits to the Philippines. These benefits had lasting effects and laid the foundation for many of the industries and structures that continue to sustain the country today.

※

UPON HEARING OF the revolutionary Katipunan movement, the Visayans wasted no time in demonstrating their loyalty to Spain. The Visayans knew that their future was tied to that of Spain and were determined to protect it at all costs. They signed manifestos, unequivocally pledging their allegiance to the Spanish Crown and denouncing the rebellious actions of the Katipuneros. The Visayans saw the Katipunan as a threat to the stability and progress brought about by Spanish rule. They condemned the movement for its ingratitude, treachery, and misguided actions:

> [They are] siding with a Satanist, non-Catholic nation that was out to grab their land and resources out of pure greed and would, therefore, end up enslaving them in the long run, the moment the Spanish forces pulled out and returned back to their European homeland.

As predicted, the departure of the Spanish forces from the Philippines marked the beginning of a long and bloody war. The Americans, who were supposed to be allies of the Tagalog Katipuneros under Aguinaldo's República de Filipinas, ended up provoking them. The Philippine-American War lasted for years and claimed the lives of as many as three million Filipinos, according to author Gore Vidal. Meanwhile, Emilio Aguinaldo and Dolores Luna, wife of Joaquín Luna y Novicio

In Iloilo City of the 1850s, a new industry emerged under the guidance of Spanish colonial rulers. Through the labor of chinos cristianos, large-scale textile manufacturing was introduced, leading to Iloilo's transformation into the textile capital of the Philippines. But this success did not occur in isolation. It was the culmination of a long-standing Spanish economic policy, initiated in the 1770s, aimed at encouraging the production of cash crops.

of Namacpacan, La Union, claimed that the República's treasury was emptied of its gold and silver reserves worth over one hundred billion U.S. dollars. The war left a devastating impact on the Philippines and its people, a legacy that continues to be felt to this day.

In the second half of the 1850s, the Visayans proved to be a success story for Spain, earning the loyalty of the Ylongos and the Cebuanos. Meanwhile, the Tagalog Katipunan revolution ended empty-handed when the Americans took away their chance of victory, making the Philippines a client state of the United States. José Rizal ultimately denounced the revolution as absurd.

It is evident that the Visayans were not influenced by the anti-friar, Masonic writings of Rizal, whose root cause was the ejection case filed against him and his family by the Dominican Order. They worked for their progress and culture, free from the conflicts between the liberal Spanish Masons and the católicos cerrados Spanish Conservatives. They wanted nothing to do with the sectarian politics that emanated from Manila. When the Americans attacked Aguinaldo's República and sent the *USS Petrel* to bombard Iloilo, the Visayans linked arms with Aguinaldo to face the American invaders. Their support for Aguinaldo came after the surrender of Spanish forces in Baler (Tayabas) to Aguinaldo and General Martín Teófilo Delgado and his Voluntarios in Iloilo.

The Ylongos and the Cebuanos must tell their independent history to counter the false narrative propagated by the Abakada puristas in their internal colonization drive over non-Tagalogs.

CHAPTER VII
YLONGOS SHUNNED 'MASONIC' KATIPUNAN

Several distinguished Jareños from different clans, which included such notable surnames as Jalandoni, Justiniani, Jereos, Javelona, Jiménez, Ledesma, Villalobos, Arguelles, González, Escarilla, Santibañez, and López, issued a signed manifesto professing their loyalty to Spain while condemning the "misguided Tagalog ingrates." The manifesto was published on September 7, 1896, in *El Porvenir de Visayas* after news of the *actos de rebelión* of a small group of Tagalog Masons known as the "Katipunan" reached Jaro and Iloilo.

The deeply Catholic Jareños were outraged upon learning of the treacherous acts of the Tagalog Katipunan Masons and their attack on a Spanish gunpowder garrison in San Juan del Monte, which was promptly quelled by the Spaniards. This led to a unanimous feeling of indignation among the Ylongo political and business leaders, which spread quickly.

Another manifesto was also signed on the same day and published in the same newspaper, led by Don Victorino Mapa, then the mayor (alcalde) of la Ciudad de Iloilo, who later became a justice of the Supreme Court during the American regime. He was of *chino cristiano* descent from the Parián de Molo.

Venancio Concepción

A ranking officer of the Batallón de Voluntarios Ylongos and of *chino cristiano* lineage, Venancio Concepción, was also a signatory to this and other manifestos for Spain. When the Voluntarios were integrated into Aguinaldo's army, he became a general who fought the Americans, not the Spaniards, during the Philippine-American War.

Don Félix de la Rama, a prominent real estate and shipping magnate and hacendero of Spanish and Chinese roots, was another significant signatory. The De la Rama family was a symbol of prosperity in Iloilo. However, the clan faced misfortune when one of its members' marriage to an American woman led to his financial ruin after she left him for another American carpetbagger. The scandalized conservative Ylongo society continues to recall this incident as a cautionary tale about the economic mismanagement of colonial mentality.

After the signing of the Pact of Biacnabató, Filipino revolutionary leaders were exiled to Hong Kong, and they gathered for a photograph. Emilio Aguinaldo can be seen positioned in the second row, fourth from the left.

In a broader sense, the Philippines suffered a similar fate at the hands of American colonizers, who portrayed themselves as benefactors but ultimately turned the country into a client state. The Americans glossed over the atrocities they committed during the Philippine-American War, leaving many Filipinos confused about their revolutionary history.

※

THE CONFLICT BETWEEN the Filipinos and Americans was downplayed in textbooks as a mere insurrection for several decades. The full extent of the people's suffering was purposefully played down to render the conflict as a vague concept in people's minds, thereby stripping it of its power to evoke anger and other emotions against the oppressors. Local U.S. propaganda utilized the public school system to teach our schoolchildren that the Philippine-American War never existed. History teachers only talked about the revolution against Spain but barely discussed the brutal Philippine-American War.

The war of resistance against the so-called "benevolent" American invaders was labeled as nothing more than an insurrection, and the Filipino participants in it as nothing but "insurrectos" or "ladrones." The Katipuneros were promoted as heroes for standing up to the local Spanish government and the Spanish

Andrés Bonifacio

religious institutions. This obfuscation resulted in Filipinos vaguely understanding the conflict as a continuing war against Spain.

❧

FOR OVER A century now, our underpaid public school history teachers have been parroting a falsity in the classroom. Until perhaps recently, our history students were never taught that the Katipunan uprising against Spain started with a failed attempt by Andrés Bonifacio to take over the polvorín of San Juan del Monte. This failure sent Bonifacio packing to Cavite, where he became a divisive figure, irreparably fracturing the Caviteño Katipunan into two factions: the "Magdiwang" and the "Magdalo." Nick Joaquín referred to this retreat as alsa balutan, which is not depicted in our history books.

In college, students are informed about the intense intramural fight between the two factions, respectively led by people allied with Bonifacio and with Aguinaldo. However, the tragic result of this conflict is vaguely narrated, with Magdalo declared as the winning faction that ordered the quick trial and execution of the Bonifacio brothers in Mount Buntis. This portrayal maligned Aguinaldo as a "traitor," while Bonifacio was consecrated as a "hero" and even reinvented as "the first president of the Philippines" by today's Philippine Freemasonry.

What is sad is that the incompetent teaching of this bloody and Masonic chapter of the prelude to the Philippine-American War is purposely being played down to bury the exact reasons behind this Bonifacio-Aguinaldo dispute. The vagueness of it further brings forth the provocative and bold assertion made by Glenn Anthony May, an American history professor and author of books on Southeast Asia and the Philippines. He asserted that an invented hero like Bonifacio is being mistakenly honored by an "ignorant generation of Filipinos influenced by American and Filipino Masonry."

Moreover, there is no substantive discussion on the real implications of the Pact of Biacnabató between Spain and the Aguinaldo-led República de Filipinas that later resisted the American invasion of this country. This pact was an important milestone because it ended Aguinaldo's revolution against Spain and led to his exile in Hong Kong in exchange for amnesty and eight hundred thousand Spanish pesos lining up his pockets and those of his trusted men.

What strengthened that same República de Filipinas against the Americans was the integration into its roster of the Ylongo and the Cebuano Visayan Voluntarios Leales, together with the other non-Tagalog Voluntarios for Spain from Luzon and Mindanao. However, our history lessons are almost entirely silent on the armed pressure brought to bear upon Aguinaldo in Cavite by the Ylongo Voluntarios and the Cebuano Leales, who joined forces with Spanish soldiers. Their combat participation helped persuade him to sign the Pacto de Biacnabató. He put down his arms for some indemnity funds from the local Spanish government, headed by Governor-General Primo de Rivera, and left for Hong Kong under the pretext that he "needed [a] rest." The Pact of Biacnabató ended the revolution against Spain even before the arrival of the Americans in this country.

❦

AGUINALDO'S STAY IN Hong Kong marked the beginning of the Philippine-American War, for all intents and purposes, as it was there where the seeds of his eventual betrayal by the Americans were planted. It is rumored that both American and British spies contacted Aguinaldo in Hong Kong, but if true, it was only because the American aggressors required the cooperation of Filipino leaders to defeat the Spanish forces in Manila.

U.S. Admiral George Dewey

General Emilio Aguinaldo

The Americans lured Aguinaldo into thinking that they would support his cause for independence from Spain in exchange for his help in Manila. They knew that if Aguinaldo's army turned against them, their campaign to conquer the Philippines would become more complex and costly. After winning Aguinaldo over, they asked him to return to Manila to harass the Spanish forces. However, when more American forces arrived, they no longer required Aguinaldo's assistance. The American forces provoked the Filipinos, and the Ylongo Voluntarios, Cebu Leales, and Balangiga rebels came together to fight against them under Aguinaldo's leadership.

Armed hostilities broke out in many parts of the archipelago, and although Aguinaldo was captured and detained, the fight was continued by Macario Sacay, who took over the presidency after General Miguel Malvar's surrender. The Americans declared victory after Malvar had surrendered, claiming to have "pacified" the country. However, some young Filipinos still lack an understanding of this simple sequence of events. This can be attributed to the flawed educational system that emphasizes rote memorization of historical events based on U.S. propaganda rather than critical thinking.

This artist's depiction captures the dramatic moment when General Emilio Aguinaldo was seized by American forces under the leadership of General Frederick Funston on March 23, 1901, in Palanan, Isabela. The scene portrays Aguinaldo and his men caught off guard and entirely surprised by the American raid. The Macabebe scouts played a crucial role in aiding the Americans during the operation.

❧

ALTHOUGH A SMALL group of Tagalog Masons were influenced by American Masons to become traitorous spies and filibusters against Spain, the Visayans and Mindanaoans remained loyal and did not plan any armed revolt. They knew that such an adventure would be futile and that Spain would eventually be forced to leave the Philippines. The Ilustrados also knew that Spain was losing the war in Cuba and that negotiations for the peace Treaty of Paris were underway. Thus, an informal arrangement was established between the departing Spanish forces and their loyal Filipino allies to protect those who would be left behind in the Philippines.

During the first week of November 1898, Visayan sugar barons, such as Don Aniceto Lacson y Ledesma and General Juan Anacleto Araneta y Torres ("Tan Juan" or Capitán Juan), pretended to stage revolts in Bago, Talisay, and Silay. Surely, these were only mock uprisings, as only a garrison of eight Spanish soldiers remained in Silay town. When the Spaniards surrendered upon the request of lawyer Don Emilio Villanueva, they were declared deserters, as they refused to return to Spain, opting instead to stay with their native Visayan wives and children.

The supposed uprisings against Spain did not, in fact, happen, as there were then no Spanish forces left in the Visayas. Furthermore, the Katipunan never had a significant influence among the Ylongos and Cebuanos, as they were prepared as independent people by their Hispanic heritage and soul. The Katipunan concept was only introduced to Visayans during the American regime through the reorganized school system, which revised Philippine history to suit their colonial agenda.

The Katipunan revolution was not unanimous nor national in scope, and only a totalitarian version of Philippine history has perpetuated this myth. The Visayans and Mindanaoans did not actively participate in the movement, and the revisionisms foisted by the present school policy will fail due to its sheer idiocy.

❧

PEPE ALAS, ALSO known as José Mario Alas y Soriano, a passionate hispanista and writer, recently published an article entitled "What Makes a Hero?" In this article, he calls into question Onofre D. Córpuz' contradictory statement about the Katipunan. How could the Katipunan be both Christian and a rebellious Masonic underground organization at the same time?

With a single blow, Pepe Alas' logic and common sense completely dismantle Córpuz' entire book, *The Roots of the Filipino Nation*, along with its misguided author. Furthermore, this exposes the spying Masonic Katipunan and its so-called patriotic revolution against Spain as a fraud. The Katipunan is revealed as nothing more than a Masonic and U.S. tool, as evidenced in Paul A. Fisher's book *Behind the Lodge Door* (pp. 211 and 212). As previously mentioned, at the turn of the twentieth century, the U.S. had imperialistic ambitions and coveted Spanish colonies, including the Philippines.

The infiltration of the Katipunan by Masons, who were mostly spies for the American invaders, is a historical fact that cannot be denied. In 1899, the Katipunan was to the invading Americans what pre-war Japanese merchants were to the Japanese forces in 1941. The Japanese fifth column arrived ahead of the invading Japanese army disguised as gardeners and street vendors selling mongo con hielo. Similarly, the Katipuneros arrived as Masons with their lodges connected to the American mother lodge, and even the Spanish Gran Oriente Lodge was connected to the Charleston American Lodge.

The Katipunan and its members were regarded as mere factotums, carrying out the bidding of opportunistic benefactors who sought to exploit their skills and services. Only an American colonial Masonic propaganda front could have unilaterally imposed a false history of our country on generations of supposedly English-educated Filipinos who, in turn, naively, if not foolishly, think that they are "surely correct" in this matter.

Pepe Alas' incisive article is hard to refute because it is true. Today's tyrants aim to suppress the freedom of historical truth because it exposes their venality and ongoing treachery to what is truly Filipino.

In his controversial article, Pepe Alas highlights the reality of the situation: The Katipunan was not a patriotic organization. It was a Masonic tool of the American colonialists, which explains why it was Masonic in character and why most of its members were Masons. It was also a spying organization, tasked to gather information on the activities of the Spanish authorities

A Filipino and a Spanish soldier pose for a studio photograph in Manila.

and report it to the American would-be invaders. Its true nature and purpose were exposed when its leaders surrendered to the Americans in exchange for a comfortable life in their new colonial government:

> Many years ago, while rummaging through costly books in one popular bookstore, I found for the first time Dr. Onofre Córpuz' famous work, *The Roots of the Filipino Nation*. I didn't have money then, so I just leafed through the pages. On page 223 (of volume II), I found a commentary of his about...the Katipunan. On that page, Córpuz wrote that this time-honored 'revolutionary group' was 'the first active embodiment of the Christian Filipino nation.'
>
> During that time, I had just reconverted to the Catholic Church (after a couple of years of toying around with godlessness and other 'isms'). My zeal back then toward the faith of my forefathers was freshly strong, and so I immediately sensed—with much chagrin—that there was something disturbingly wrong with Dr. Córpuz' assertion. I asked myself, how could someone like him, a giant in the academe, had written something as incomprehensible as the Katipunan embodying a Christian nation when that group was an offshoot of Freemasonry? As many Dan Brown-educated kids should know by now, Freemasonry is the ancient enemy of the Church. As a Christian student of history, I was deeply intrigued by the extent of the late Dr. Córpuz' knowledge about the role of Freemasonry during those tumultuous final years of our country's history under Spain. However, was Dr. Córpuz unaware of the Katipunan's Masonic roots and motives? I find it hard to believe that. Or did he leave that fact out conveniently because he was a Freemason himself, or perhaps its sympathizer? But if he was, wouldn't it still be ridiculous for a Mason to say that a violent group who tortured and chopped off the heads of friars just because they were Spaniards embodied the Christian Filipino nation?
>
> To those still unaware, Freemasonry has been condemned numerous times by the Catholic Church. To my knowledge, there had been at least 24 papal pronouncements regarding this matter (perhaps the most famous was Pope Leo XIII's papal encyclical *Humanum Genus*, which was released in 1884). As one of the best academicians our country [has] ever had, it strikes me as odd why Dr. Córpuz failed to emphasize the Masonic origins of the Katipunan in his controversial conclusion. A little research will show that the Katipunan's third and final Supremo, Andrés Bonifacio (you read that right: he wasn't the first), joined the Logia Taliba (No. 165) and from there imbibed his radical and anti-friar ideas. Bonifacio also joined Rizal's Liga Filipina in 1892. The group was, in fact, a Masonic lodge in the making (or was it already?). These organizations, not to mention their members, were hardly Christian if we view them from a Catholic lens.
>
> After the failure of the Liga Filipina and the arrest and deportation of Rizal to Dapitan, the campaign for peaceful reforms hit a [brick wall]. Thus, an

agitated and disenchanted Marcelo H. del Pilar, himself a high-ranking Mason and a rabid propagandista who had been on self-exile in Spain for years, wrote to his brother-in-law, Deodato Arellano, and urged the latter to form a much more radical and violent group to end Spain's reign in Filipinas finally. Arellano thus gathered other members of the beleaguered Liga to form the Katipunan (yes, it was Arellano, and not Bonifacio, who founded the Katipunan as instigated by del Pilar).

When government forces discovered the existence of the Katipunan in late 1896, what happened next was bloodshed and the senseless killing and torture of innocent Spanish friars and other individuals who went against the Katipuneros' way. Did ordinary civilians welcome the 'revolution' participated mostly by Tagalogs? No, they didn't. Life went on for most Filipinos living far from where the action was. No national sentiment supported the Katipunan rebellion against Spain (see *One Woman's Liberating: The Life and Career of Estefanía Aldaba-Lim* by Nick Joaquín).

Pepe Alas, author of "El Filipinismo" blog.

It should be noted in the preceding paragraph that the Katipunan was discovered by accident. Keep in mind that it was an underground organization. Simply put, the Katipunan was an ILLEGAL ASSOCIATION, no matter how hard one tries to paint it with dainty colors of patriotism and love of country.

One might say it had lofty ideals of freedom and nationhood, thus excusing it from illegalities. But so do the Moro Islamic Liberation Front and the Abu Sayyaf, who try to picture themselves as the martyrs of their delusional Bangsamoro. Should we consider them heroes too?

...Seeing now that the Katipunan was a bastard child of Freemasonry, the ancient enemy of the Christian religion, how in the world did Dr. Córpuz come up with the idea that the Katipunan was the first active embodiment of the Christian Filipino nation?

The Katipuneros made incisions in their arms to sign membership papers using their blood. They swore loyalty to the Katipunan in front of a human skull. They swore to kill even members of their own families for the sake of the Katipunan's secrecy. Where is Christianity in all that?

This is not to say that Bonifacio was an evil man; only God can judge whether he was, despite the many friars he had shamed and ordered tortured and killed, and churches burned and desecrated. Going beyond the rebellion, we will never know much about his character, for he was not as chronicled as Rizal. For all we know, Bonifacio could have been a virtuous man. Nevertheless, that is not the point. Whatever personal distinction he may have had was not why we now have several monuments for him, nor was it why we commemorate his birthday every November 30.

On February 16, 1921, the Philippine Legislature, under the auspices of U.S. Governor-General Francis Burton Harrison, enacted Act No. 2946, making November 30 of each year a legal holiday to commemorate the birth of Bonifacio. The holiday has since been known as Bonifacio Day, making the Katipunan [leader] a Filipino national hero....It is, of course, difficult to accept that Bonifacio should be removed from our pantheon of heroes....

Pepe Alas questions the idea of tyranny that has been taught to him all his life, as no one has been able to accurately define it. He argues that Spain created the country and united different tribes under one language, government, and faith to prevent them from warring against each other. He asks where the tyranny is in this situation and points out that they were given schools and universities. He acknowledges that not all Spanish officials and friars during the Empire days were just, but argues that the promises of Freemasonry inspired rebellion and violence, without bringing true freedom.

> Was Spain tyrannical when it shipped to our country countless items (tomato, calendar, piano, wheat, books, polo, pantalón, chico, bougainvillea, violin, watermelon, guava, printing press, etcetera) and [introduced] concepts (chivalry, palabra de honor, philosophy, law, land ownership, Western art, age/birthday, Christianity, etcetera) that have made us what we are today—as Filipinos? We adore old mementos from our past (bahay na bató, traditions, etcetera) and decry their dwindling number and alarming disappearance. But such mementos were from the hated Spanish period. So why bother saving and conserving them if they all come from such a tyrannical era?

> We all miss our grandfathers who used to bring us to Church on Sundays and carry us on their shoulders so that we could see the saints' processions from above a thick crowd; we all miss our grandmothers who never tired praying the rosary day and night. All these are vestiges from that tyrannical period. Why bother missing them at all?

He also casts doubt on the idea of organizing stealth groups to undermine the government, and instead suggests focusing on actions that could uplift the lives of Filipinos. He concludes that Bonifacio's actions led to bloodshed and the downfall of what Spain had built for centuries and urges that instead of commemorating him as a hero, we should focus on creating lasting and meaningful changes for the Filipino people.

> We have had so much distrust toward our government. From Ferdinand Marcos to President Rodrigo Duterte. Shouldn't we all follow the Katipune-

Onofre D. Córpuz

ros of old and organize stealth groups to undermine the present government for freedom?

If I used the hashtag #NotAHero, it would be appropriate to attach it to that Masonically misled man from Tondo whose birthday we methodically commemorate today because instead of thinking of something that would have genuinely helped and uplifted the lives of the unfortunate Filipino masses of his time—by establishing something such as the Kadiwa Public Market, for instance—Bonifacio brought bloodshed instead, which led not only to his death but also to the downfall of what Spain had strongly forged for over three centuries.

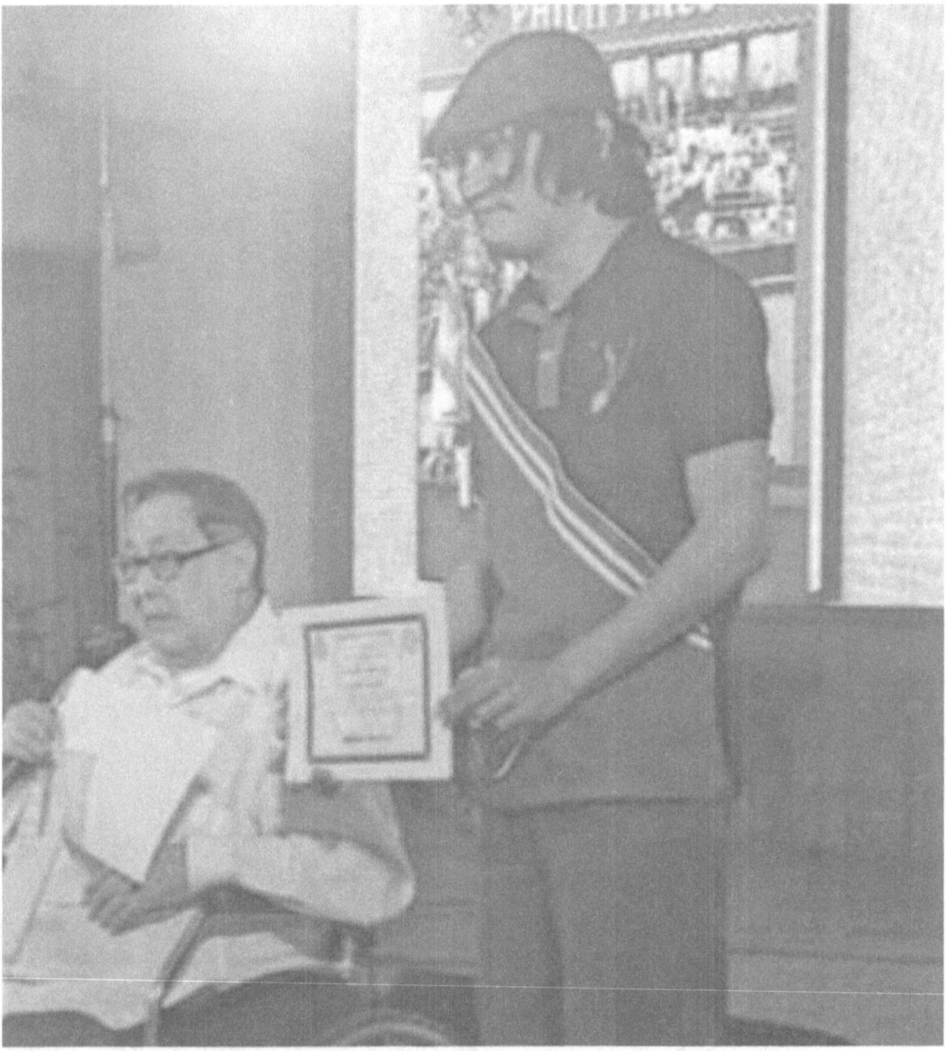

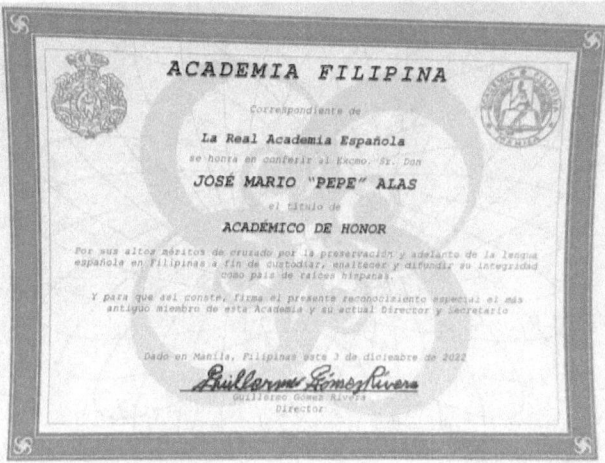

ACADEMIA FILIPINA

Correspondiente de

La Real Academia Española

se honra en conferir al Excmo. Sr. Don

JOSÉ MARIO "PEPE" ALAS

el título de

ACADÉMICO DE HONOR

Por sus altos méritos de cruzado por la preservación y adelanto de la lengua española en Filipinas a fin de custodiar, enaltecer y difundir su integridad como país de raíces hispanas.

Y para que así conste, firma el presente reconocimiento especial el más antiguo miembro de esta Academia y su actual Director y Secretario

Dado en Manila, Filipinas este 3 de diciembre de 2022

Guillermo Gómez Rivera

Guillermo Gómez Rivera
Director

Guillermo Gómez Rivera, the director of the Academia Filipina de la Real Academia Española, poses with José Mario "Pepe" Alas shortly after Alas' induction as an honorary member of the academy in December 2022. Alas was admitted into the academy for his efforts to preserve the Spanish language in the Philippines through his writings on various social media platforms.

CHAPTER VIII
INVENTING HEROES TO CONFUSE HISTORY

The art of war propaganda and public relations techniques have been mastered by the Americans to mislead and confuse their target audiences, including schoolchildren and adolescents, to advance U.S. "national interests" worldwide, particularly in the Philippines. This form of neocolonialism extends its reach even to social studies and history textbooks, which have negative impacts on both teachers and students. This propaganda follows the same old U.S. colonial agenda that was primarily developed by biased American historians Emma Helen Blaire and James Alexander Robertson, and the contentious American official Dean C. Worcester, who gained notoriety with the publication of the 1908 "Aves de rapiña" editorial and the Lapu-lapu monument controversy of 1915.

Considering this background, it's not shocking that Visayan history has been misrepresented, especially when it comes to the Ylongo Voluntarios between 1896-98, the Cebuano Leales for Spain, and the gruesome Balangiga massacre of Filipino males over ten years old in 1901.

Today, the "official history" written by Americanized historians like Teodoro A. Agoncillo and purista Abakadista linguists and writers like Lope K. Santos has been weaponized to indoctrinate our innocent children under the guise of "education" to portray the U.S. as a friend, despite its record of exploiting the Philippines to further its national interests.

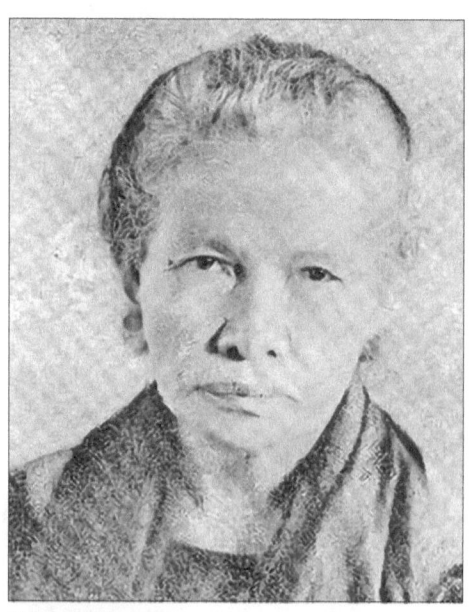
Teresa Magbanua

For instance, it's a known fact that Visayans, particularly the Ylongos and Cebuanos, never revolted against Spain. Nevertheless, there are stories of a Joan of Arc of the Visayas, Teresa Magbanua from Pototan, Iloilo, who allegedly led soldiers in a battle against Spain in Pototan. However, a closer look at her biography reveals that Magbanua fought against the invading Americans and not the Spanish forces under Governor-General Diego de los Ríos, who had already surrendered to the Voluntarios and the Estado Federal de Visayas. Nonetheless, people still refer to her as the "Joan of Arc of the Visayas" who fought the Spaniards.

Another case of deliberate historical distortion is that of Capitán Epifanio de la Concepción from Iloilo. He was erroneously labeled a revolutionary against Spain, which is untrue. We know for a fact he was an Ylongo Voluntario for Spain because he was our maternal granduncle. We also know another Voluntario named José Rivera, who was our maternal grandfather. Lourdes Rivera y Celo, our biological mother, was José Rivera's eldest daughter. Incidentally, he was the first American-appointed mayor (presidente) of the town, now city, of Passi, Iloilo province.

Gliceria Marella

Don Epifanio wrote a book that provided a retrospective and detailed account of his time with the Ylongo Voluntarios. His book sheds light on how these "voluntarios" later became "revolucionarios," even though they never rebelled against Spain. What happened was that after the Spanish forces had left the Visayas, these voluntarios joined Aguinaldo's army to fight against the American invaders. Therefore, they were revolutionaries against the Americans but not the Spaniards, as the "official history" taught in schools would have us believe.

※

ANOTHER INDIVIDUAL WHO is often likened to Joan of Arc is Doña Gliceria Marella of Taal, Batangas. Unlike the famous French heroine, Doña Gliceria did not lead an army to battle against Spanish forces, but instead financed a "Maluya" battalion with arms and ammunition. She was negotiating for the release of her sick husband, Don Eulalio, who had been arrested for being a Mason sympathizer of Aguinaldo's army. While she did not engage in combat, she endured a different kind of struggle against the invading Americans, who caused more deaths and hardships to the Batangueños than the inferior Spanish forces ever did. The American invaders brought cholera, typhoid, and dysentery epidemics that killed more Tagalogs in a few months than the Spaniards did in over three hundred years, as documented in Glenn May's *The Battle of Batangas*.

In Bohol, a man who died in a duel was denied entry to a church and funeral services by a Jesuit parish priest. This angered Francisco Dagohoy, the deceased's

The National Historical Commission of the Philippines has revised the romanticized image of Lapu-lapu propagated by American-era propaganda against Spain. Historian Danilo Gerona's fresh findings reveal that Lapu-lapu was actually an older man with flabby skin and a slightly stooped figure (right), contrary to the virile, muscular warrior image (left) that was used to demonize Magellan and the Spaniards.

brother, to the point that he killed the priest at the church entrance, although the priest was only doing his job. Under Church law, anyone killed in a duel is indirectly guilty of self-murder, as they risked their life for no justifiable reason.

Francisco Dagohoy

The guardias civiles were sent to arrest the killer, who fled and hid in the mountains to evade punishment. However, American-influenced historians have depicted the priest killer, Dagohoy, as a Bohol hero who rebelled against Spain for over eighty years. This is a deception, as Dagohoy was not a rebel but a madman who lost his senses. The Spaniards had nothing to do with his crime, and it is illogical to make him a hero, much like calling gangster Al Capone a hero because he rebelled against American society.

In the case of Lapu-lapu, an American colonizer named Dean C. Worcester erected a monument in Punta Engaño, Mactan, in 1915. Worcester made a hero out of Lapu-lapu, portraying him as a muscular young man who killed Magellan, despite the majority of Cebuano Catholics objecting to this mischaracterization. The Cebuanos were thankful to Magellan for introducing them to the first Cross, the first Mass, and the Santo Niño. However, Worcester spread fake news that Lapu-lapu killed Magellan in hand-to-hand combat, despite historical evidence to the contrary. This hoax has been taught to generations of schoolchildren, perpetuating the lie.

Lastly, the case of Bonifacio, another supposed hero, is called into question. After Bonifacio failed to capture the San Juan del Monte gunpowder depot, he fled to Cavite. There, the political rivalry between him and Aguinaldo resulted in his and his brother Procopio's execution on Mount Buntis by Filipino revolutionaries, not by the Spanish Manila authorities. This flaw in the Katipunan narrative proves that unadulterated Ylongo and Cebuano history should be given more credibility as it is more faithful to the truth.

CHAPTER IX
SPAIN SAYS 'ADIOS' TO LOYAL YLONGOS

Under the leadership of the last Spanish governor-general of the Philippines, Diego de los Ríos, there was a loyal aide by his side, Don Ricardo Monet, who served as the politico-military governor of Iloilo, and by extension, of the Visayas and Mindanao. After American Admiral George Dewey successfully took control of Manila, De los Ríos and Monet made the strategic decision to move the capital of the Spanish Philippines to Iloilo. It was Monet who had the foresight to organize the Ylongo Voluntarios, and he appointed Don Martín Teófilo Delgado, the municipal judge of Santa Bárbara at the time, as commander.

When a ceasefire was established after Manila was captured, Spain knew that their economically struggling nation was no match for the superior forces of the United States. Despite this realization, Spain continued to fight in Cuba, where the majority of the conflict took place. In 1896, before the war broke out, José Rizal, who was exiled in Dapitan, volunteered to serve as a doctor for the Spanish army in Cuba. The war between the U.S. and Spain, which aimed to capture Cuba, Puerto Rico, and Filipinas, lasted just over three months in 1898. However, the Ylongo Voluntarios and the Cebuano Leales had been organized to

Uniformed Ylongo Voluntarios converge at Plaza Alfonso XII (Plaza Libertad) on Christmas Day in 1898 for a solemn send-off ceremony. The last remaining Spanish forces are about to embark on a journey to Zamboanga en route to their home country of Spain, marking a momentous event.

fight for their country, Spain, since the early 1890s.

The Katipunan uprising, led by a group of Tagalog Masons headed by Andrés Bonifacio, proved irrelevant when they failed to capture the Spanish gunpowder depot in San Juan del Monte, known as El Polvorín. As a result, Bonifacio fled to Cavite, where the República Filipina under Aguinaldo eventually arrested and tried him and his brother Procopio for treason, sentencing them to death in Maragondon. The Manila Military Court, known as the Tribunal de Guerra, ordered the arrest of the Masons, including José Rizal, who was accused of "illicit association and rebellion." However, Rizal was dragged into this mess by the Katipunan, who claimed him as their leader. All twenty or more witnesses against Rizal before the military court were members of the Katipunan, who were known to Manila authorities as Masons spying for the United States.

Brigadier General Ricardo Monet

As De los Ríos and Monet foresaw the defeat of Spain, they also knew that their local Voluntario forces were waiting for the signing of the Treaty of Paris before declaring themselves revolutionaries. After all, the local Spanish forces under De los Ríos and Monet had already prepared to leave Iloilo for Zamboanga and go to Spain. With this looming reality, it was even said that Brigadier General Monet instructed Spanish mestizo Delgado to declare that the Voluntarios had turned "revolucionarios" against Spain, which Delgado did after explaining the strategy to his followers.

This strategic move aimed to confuse the invading Americans, who would later hail and respect the Ylongo Voluntarios as a heroic army against Spain, even after the Spaniards had already departed in peace and on amicable terms with their Voluntario forces, as well as with the general civilian population of Iloilo, Molo, and Jaro. On Christmas Day, December 25, 1898, at six o'clock in the morning, the Ylongo Voluntarios, dressed in their uniform de rayadillo cubano provided by the Spanish government, massed at Jaro Plaza, where they started their triumphal march toward Iloilo's Plaza Alfonso XII. The Spanish forces would turn over Iloilo City and the entire country to the Voluntarios.

Just a day before, the last capital of the Spanish empire in the Orient was handed over by Governor-General De los Ríos to the Ylongo Voluntarios, marking an end to over three hundred years of Spanish dominance in the country. This momentous event occurred nearly a month prior to Aguinaldo's proclamation as president in Malolos on January 23, 1899.

On Christmas day, the people of Jaro flocked to the expansive Plaza de Jaro and surrounding streets. They erupted in thunderous applause and cried out "¡Viva España!" with tears streaming down their faces. Word had spread throughout the town that the Voluntarios were set to rendezvous with the Spanish troops, led by General Monet, who would sign the acta de capitulación (deed of surrender) to the Filipino forces.

Days earlier, on December 16, General Ananías Diokno from Batangas arrived in Capiz aboard a ship generously donated by Gliceria Marella from Taal. This Tagalog unit, dispatched by Aguinaldo, was en route to Iloilo, where they would soon be joined by the Ylongo Voluntarios under the banner of Aguinaldo's República de Filipinas.

※

Governor-General Diego de los Ríos

AS THE DEPARTING Spanish forces lined up in formation, the Ylongo Voluntarios led by Delgado and Adriano Hernández, as well as prominent citizens of Iloilo, gathered to witness the historic moment. General Monet, heading the Spanish forces, presented them with the deed of surrender, while delivering a speech that moved everyone present to tears. Spain was bidding farewell to the people of Iloilo, wishing them all the best as they deserved freedom and independence.

The womenfolk of Ylongo could not contain their emotions and began to wail, as the señoras and older men wept silently. Even the young men joined the Voluntarios in formation as they cried out, "¡Viva España!"

General Monet expressed gratitude for the loyalty demonstrated by the Ylongos toward Spain, as he delivered a speech that was filled with emotion and appreciation:

> We are going away because we lost the war, but we thank you, Ylongos, Visayos, and Filipinos, for siding with us. God will protect you because you are a grateful and noble people. We turn over to you a prosperous country and a noble and civilized people. We turn over to you this city, this province,

THE INDEPENDENT HISTORY OF YLONGO AND CEBUANO VISAYANS 73

At the peak of the Spanish-American War, a group of Spanish officers and infantrymen appears on camera in Manila.

rich in resources and splendid in its infrastructure. Spain will always be your Mother country. Adios!

With hearts full of pride and eyes brimming with tears, the Spanish forces bid farewell to their Filipino counterparts, the Voluntarios, as they marched in unison toward the crowded wharf, ready to board their ships bound for Zamboanga. It was a momentous occasion, marked by embraces and well wishes for the future.

Delgado declared that Plaza Alfonso XII would be forever known as "Plaza Libertad"—a fitting tribute to the hard-fought victory for independence.

But the winds of change were already blowing, and just over a month later, an American task force, led by Brigadier General Marcus P. Miller, arrived in the Iloilo Straight. With brazen confidence, they demanded the city's surrender, which the proud Voluntarios fiercely refused.

What followed was a brutal and devastating conflict, with American shelling raining down upon the city, causing many casualties, which the invaders dismissively labeled as "half-breed Chinese and Spanish bandits." The Ylongos and the Tagalogs in Iloilo bravely joined forces, determined to protect their homeland from foreign occupation, even as more American foot soldiers arrived on the shores of Iloilo, igniting a protracted war that would forever alter the course of history.

CHAPTER X
ANTI-SPANISH MANILA SHOULD BE OPPOSED

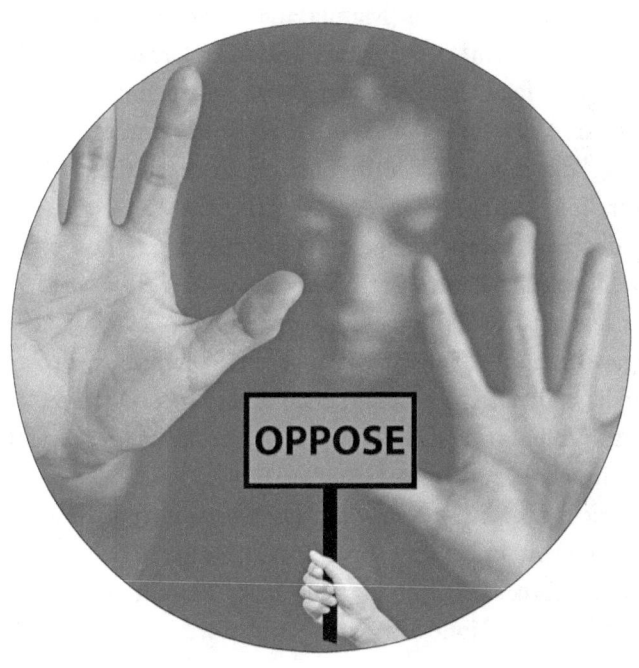

It is a common misconception that the Katipunan revolution was a national uprising. However, the presence of Voluntarios among Tagalogs, Pampangos, Bicolanos, and Mindanaoans suggests otherwise. In fact, the Visayans formed volunteer brigades to fight for Spain, and only declared independence after the Spanish forces had surrendered and left Iloilo.

Anton Paas, a writer from Mindanao, confirms that the only Katipunan-related uprising in Mindanao happened in the Iligan Fort in Lanao. This uprising involved convicted criminals from Manila and other parts of Luzon who claimed to be members of the Manila Katipunan. Manuel Corrales, a leading Cagayanon during that time, described these Katipuneros as "the criminals of the worst kind."

The Cagayan Voluntarios and other Spanish forces were able to stop the Katipunan "disciplinario" criminals from reaching Cagayan de Misamis. However, like their Ylongo counterparts, the Cagayan and Misamis Voluntarios only declared independence eight months after the defeat of Rear Admiral Patricio Montojo y Pasarón at Manila Bay, and only when it became clear that Spain was leaving the Philippines for good.

Zamboanga, the most loyalist bastion of the Voluntarios, declared its friendly and peaceful independence from Spain about a year after Montojo's defeat. Meanwhile, the Davao Voluntarios did not declare any independence as they were still hoping that Spain would return to Davao.

These historical accounts reveal that the Visayans and Mindanaoans declared themselves independent only after Spain had already left the Philippines. The invading American forces had yet to come from Manila aboard gunboats headed by the *USS Petrel* to shell Iloilo City and Jaro before threatening Cebu to demand its surrender.

※

IT IS A LITTLE-KNOWN FACT that many Filipinos actually sided with Spain in their fight against the Katipunan, a reality that is not mentioned in Philippine history textbooks. In the pursuit of a false narrative that the Katipunan revolution was nationwide and unanimous in scope, our education policymakers have overlooked this aspect. It is worth noting that the chinos cristianos, who had businesses to protect, also did not participate in the revolt against Spain.

The truth is, only a Tagalog minority, mostly composed of Masons, came out in open rebellion after their secret revolutionary society was discovered by Spanish friar Padre Mariano Gil, the parish priest of Tondo, Manila at the time. Spanish intelligence had heard rumors about this clandestine revolutionary society for a while, but they had no solid evidence until that fateful day.

Manila had long been rife with rumors about a foreign spy network working for the interests of England, which had colonies in Malaysia and China, and was allegedly planning, along with the United States, to take over the Spanish overseas possessions, including the Philippines. Local Masons were said to be involved as spies in these plans.

The Katipunan, as revealed in the book *Behind the Lodge Door* (pp. 211, 212) by Paul A. Fisher, was actually a Masonic lodge ruled by American and English Masons who were in direct contact with Emilio Aguinaldo, giving him direction on how to stage a revolution against Spain. Aguinaldo led the revolution, but he did so as a dedicated member and tool of the Craft.

Interestingly, Freemasonry was introduced in Spain by a British nobleman, the Duke of Wharton, to destroy the Spanish empire from within. The Spaniards discovered this plot too late, and had lost almost all of their American territories in the 1820s, with only Cuba, Puerto Rico, and Filipinas remaining under their dominion.

By the 1890s, Spain saw itself under attack by Masons, and in the Philippines by the Katipunan, which was another lodge of the Gran Oriente Español. As a result, the Spanish military rounded up Filipino and Spanish Masons and had them executed by firing squad at the Luneta, including José Rizal and Francisco Roxas, a Spaniard. Roxas was publicly put to death, along with fourteen other Manila Masons.

This was reminiscent of the earlier execution of the Thirteen Martyrs of Cavite (Trece Mártires) and the fifteen so-called martyrs of Bicol, among them the Spanish Abellas. It is worth noting, however, that President Aguinaldo later repented and reconciled with Spain and the Catholic Church, as emphasized by Carlos P. Rómulo in his article "De Cavite a las Naciones Unidas," which appeared in the October 12, 1964 issue of *Hispanidad*. This magazine used to be published in Manila. Aguinaldo, like Rizal, also gave up Freemasonry shortly before his death by receiving Holy Communion and the last rites.

CELIA DÍAZ LAUREL, the late artist and widow of former Vice President Salvador H. Laurel, devoted a whole chapter in her book about her grandfather, Domingo Franco y Tuáson, entitled *The Masons*, where she dissected their role in the Spanish-American War in Cuba, Puerto Rico, and the Philippines. The swift executions of the Masons may have appeared as an abuse of power by Spanish authorities, but in reality, they were only defending themselves and the Spanish state, including its overseas provinces such as the Philippines.

Upon discovering the rules of the Katipunan, Spaniards were horrified by the brutal code that required a Katipunero to kill even his own family if they accidentally revealed the Masonic secrets of the organization. The killing of Spanish priests and missionaries by Bonifacio, a Spanish mestizo, not only angered Spanish and Filipino Catholics but also surprised and shocked even Aguinaldo, who was a Mason himself and held the highest honor of the thirty-third degree.

Similar to the New People's Army today, the Katipunan demanded revolutionary taxes from chino cristiano traders and rural farmers. Those who refused to comply were either reported as Katipunan members to the Spanish authorities or secretly murdered. During the Cry of Pugad Lawin, Bonifacio ordered the killing of as many Binondo Chinese or chino cristiano traders as possible. The wealthy bell maker Hilario Súnico was questioned by the Spanish authorities because the Katipunan had left papers and Masonic propaganda in his house, deliberately implicating him and even the low-profile Ongpins. A member of the rich and landed Roxas-Ayala clan, Don Francisco Roxas, was mistakenly executed by the authorities because he was falsely accused of being a Katipunero for refusing to participate in their illegal activities.

Rizal had complained about being framed by the Katipunan, for which he wrote a manifesto condemning them and their revolution as useless and absurd. The Katipunan also sent many spies and recruiters to Iloilo, Capiz, Aklan, and Cebu to enlist members for the Masonic Katipunan. However, the Ylongo Voluntarios stopped them and had them executed. In Cebu, León Kilát, the

León Kilát, nom de guerre of Lieutenant General Pantaleón Villegas y Soldi, killed by the Cebuano Leales for recruiting them to the Katipunan. He is now celebrated as a hero, with a monument dedicated in his honor in Carcar, Cebu, and other locations in the province.

THE INDEPENDENT HISTORY OF YLONGO AND CEBUANO VISAYANS

Katipunero leader Lieutenant General Pantaleón Villegas y Soldi, was killed by the Cebuano Leales in Carcar when he tried to recruit Cebuanos for the Katipunan. They stabbed him multiple times after welcoming him as a guest in one of the Carcar mansions. Most of the hacenderos of Carcar were chinos cristianos from the prosperous Parián de Cebu, and a Leal named Noel led in the killing of León Kilát.

Fray Maríano Gil, OSA, the friar who exposed the existence of the Katipunan.

THE HISTORY OF the Philippines has been a subject of great debate and controversy over the years, as different groups of people have tried to revise and retell events from the past to suit their own interests and agendas. One of the most egregious examples of this is the way that American invaders and Abakadistas have distorted the truth about the Visayan Voluntarios and Cebuano Leales who sided with Spain until the Americans arrived to "pacify" the Visayas.

Perhaps the most brutal incident that these revisionists have failed to acknowledge is the Balangiga massacre, which took place during the Philippine-American War in 1901. American soldiers sought to kill every Filipino male over the age of ten in the town of Balangiga out of fear that they might bear arms against the invaders and in retaliation for an attack by Filipino guerrillas. The Americans also rampaged and turned Samar into "a howling wilderness." These events highlight the devastating impact that colonialism can have on a nation and its people.

After capturing Aguinaldo and later executing his successor, Macario Sacay, in Luzon, the Americans used "education in English" as a means of subduing the future Tagalogs. They rewrote the stories of Rizal and Bonifacio to brainwash the new generation against Spain. These stories are now accepted as fact without question, and even a fictional character like Padre Dámaso in *Noli Me Tangere* is seen as the nemesis of the Filipino people. Sadly, this has resulted in a lack of understanding of the real enemies of the Philippines, such as Dean C. Worcester of the American colonial period and present-day Tagalog puristas.

The Visayans, especially the Ylongos, had a vastly different experience during the Spanish colonial period. They were able to avoid much of the trouble and conflict that plagued other regions, and in fact, they parted as good friends with the Spanish forces, who humbly surrendered to them. The Visayans tearfully swore eternal friendship with the Spaniards without firing a single shot before bidding them goodbye. This level-headedness and diplomacy were fully displayed in the actions of Cebuanos like Senator Vicente Yap Sotto and Congressman Miguel Cuenco, along with Samareño Congressman Pascual B. Azanza and Ylongo Senator Enrique B. Magalona, who later sponsored bills to teach and preserve Spanish in the Philippines.

However, the implementation of this law on the teaching of Spanish did not succeed, as it was stymied every step of the way by the noisy purista politicians who were determined to abolish Spanish. They inherited their Hispanophobia from the scheming English and American Masons who implanted an "educational system" in the Philippines in the early twentieth century. This misguided approach led to the unnecessary abolition of Spanish through a misinformed, ill-advised, and corrupt "Dilawan lady dictator." The purista politicians failed to recognize the value of Spanish as a tool for development, particularly in call centers. In the end, their shortsightedness and idiocy led to the downfall of this political dynasty, which had met the karmic end predicted by an 1840 prophecy that puts a maldición (curse) upon Filipino Hispanophobes.

In conclusion, it is clear that the history of the Philippines has been rewritten and retold by various groups of people over time. The Visayan experience during the Spanish colonial period was vastly different from that of the Tagalogs. The Visayans were able to maintain a peaceful and mutually respectful relationship with the Spaniards, which was based on diplomacy and mutual understanding. However, it is crucial to acknowledge all of the events that occurred during the colonial period, including the Balangiga massacre.

By learning from our past and avoiding the same mistakes in the future, we can ensure a brighter and more harmonious future for all Filipinos. It is also important to recognize the impact of language and education on our history and culture. The imposition of English by American colonizers and the subsequent purist movement against Spanish has had a significant effect on the way Filipinos view their own identity and history. The recent resurgence of interest in Spanish language and culture, particularly in the field of call centers, highlights the shortsightedness of those who sought to eradicate it from our society. As we move forward, we should strive to embrace our complex and diverse history, including the contributions and experiences of all Filipinos, in order to build a more inclusive and culturally rich nation.

In the end, our goal should be to build a society that is grounded in mutual respect, understanding, and acceptance. We must embrace our diversity and use it to our advantage, creating a society that is truly reflective of the rich cultural heritage of the Philippines. By doing so, we can ensure a brighter, more harmonious future for all Filipinos, one in which we can all take pride in our history and our shared identity as Filipinos.

Call centers in the Philippines are now seeking Spanish-speaking employees, offering higher wages compared to their English-speaking counterparts. This demand for Spanish language proficiency has led to a resurgence of interest in the language among young Filipinos looking to earn more. However, this renewed interest also exposes the short-sightedness of Filipino political leaders over the last few decades, particularly the decision made by former President Corazon C. Aquino to abolish the mandatory teaching of Spanish in schools.

… CHAPTER XI
HOW YLONGOS VIEWED
RIZAL, KKK LEADERS

Today, the photographs of Andrés Bonifacio and other Ilustrados associated with the revolution show them dressed in European attire, such as an overcoat de Americana complete with cravat or bow tie. This is not surprising since they considered themselves Europeans as Spanish subjects. However, American-influenced history textbooks depict Bonifacio in red Balintawak-dinampul pants and a transparent abaca-sinamay barong Tagalog while holding a bolo, despite no photographic evidence of him wearing such a getup. This portrayal aligns with the American neocolonial propaganda agenda, which aims to misrepresent Bonifacio as a Spanish mestizo and demonize the Spanish friars through fictional characters like Fray Salvi, Fray Camorra, and Fray Dámaso. Unfortunately, this campaign has been so successful that we have lost sight of the real colonial monsters in our national history, such as Dean C. Worcester and the "Aves de rapiña" colonialists.

On the other hand, José Rizal, a known Masonic writer, attacked and maligned the friars and the Catholic Church through satire due to his losing in an ejectment case filed against him and his family by the Dominican Spanish friars who owned the Calamba friar estate, which was leased to them. Rizal attended the University of Santo Tomás, which was founded by the Dominicans, and his attacks were more out of a "loser's" desire to avenge his family's loss in the land dispute rather than for patriotism or social reform, as taught to schoolchildren today. One interviewee described Rizal's attacks as the excuses of a deadbeat tenant ("Son escusas de mal pagador").

In 1906, a chino cristiano journalist and poet named Don Emeterio Barcelón y Barceló Soriano wrote the following in the daily newspaper *Libertas* (translated by us):

> The Dominican friars knew Rizal by the familiar name of Pepe Rizal, and they had a close relationship with him before he went to Europe. After returning from Germany [where he trained in opthalmology] from a European university, his fellow townsmen in Calamba regarded him as an oracle. He successfully spread and convinced people of his theories about the private ownership of the Calamba estate. However, Pepe Rizal forgot that without the economic support of the friars for his family, he would not have been able to study in Europe. In fact, the Dominican friars had given Don Francisco, José Rizal's father, five hundred hectares of the best hacienda lands in Calamba. These lands were already cleared and free of rent payment for the first five years of the contract (p. 195, *Sobre una reseña de Filipinas*, UST, Manila, 1907).

It is evident from this source that upon his return from Europe, Rizal, now a Mason, openly questioned the Dominican friars' ownership of their lands in Calamba. These lands had been granted to the Dominicans by the King of Spain many years ago. Rizal's sisters, Narcisa and Olimpia, had also joined Freemasonry, becoming members of the lodge headed by a Spanish mestiza, Rosario Villaruel, "La adopción semilla." Despite their privileged position as favored Dominican tenants, the Rizal siblings were aware that their affiliation with this forbidden society would be seen as a position of defiance and hostility against their lessors. When they refused to pay rent and challenged the Dominicans' ownership of the Calamba hacienda, the friars filed an ejectment case against them. Don Emeterio provides a detailed explanation of the land dispute. We have loosely translated the following text:

> Despite using kindness and patience to persuade their tenants, the Spanish Dominican Order was forced to go to court to settle their disagreement. They won the ejectment case in the Court of First Instance, but the Rizals appealed the case at the Royal Audiencia, only to have the High Court uphold the lower court's decision in favor of the lessors. Despite this ruling, the lessees refused to comply and threatened to disrupt the peace in Calamba.
>
> As a result, authorities sent fifty extra police officers to assist local judicial authorities in enforcing the law, under the command of a colonel from the Vigésimo Tercio de la Guardia Civil. However, even with this additional force, the tenants refused to vacate the premises, defying the final court order. The agents with the court sheriff were assisted by extra police forces and ordered the losing party to gather their belongings and leave the hacienda within twenty-four hours. As most of the dwellings were made of lightweight materials such as bamboo and nipa, they could be easily carried outside the hacienda. The authorities warned that failing to do so would result in the burning of these dwellings. Despite this warning, the tenants deliberately disobeyed the lawful orders, and the police authorities were forced to carry out their warning and burn these materials of bamboo and nipa.

Emeterio Barcelón y Barceló Soriano

AS THE AUTHORITIES executed the court order, the Rizal family had already vacated their Calamba mansion and transferred to Manila and Hong Kong. Twenty-five families, consisting of Rizal family farm workers, resisted the final execution order. However, they were left with no choice but to leave their homes and belongings behind as they faced the threat of having their dwellings burned down.

In a book by León Ma. Guerrero, Rizal is said to have had several meetings with the Spanish governor-general, who courteously received him several times in his palace. During these meetings, Rizal and his family expressed their desire to relocate to Sabah. However, the governor-general objected to this proposal, suggesting instead that they settle anywhere else in the Philippines, but Laguna, preferably in a place far away from the disputed Dominican hacienda.

It is interesting to note that this chapter about the Rizal ejection from Calamba is deliberately overlooked in teaching the Rizal course and Rizal biographies. Why is this the case? The answer is obvious. Including this context in history books would cast doubt on the patriotic motive of Rizal in writing against the friars and the Spanish administration policies. It would also lead to a very different story from what is being officially told today to our schoolchildren.

The real story of Rizal was known to the Ylongo Voluntarios. They sided with Spain and only coalesced with Aguinaldo's República de Filipinas after Spain had departed. The American invaders had provoked the Philippine-American War that only ended after the secret execution of Macario Sacay in 1907—the second president of the First Filipino Republic who spoke in Spanish like his Latin American counterparts.

Moreover, it is worth noting that Rizal's stance on revolution and independence is often misunderstood. While he was critical of the abuses committed by the Spanish colonizers and the friars, he also recognized the need for reform and peaceful change. He believed that the best way to achieve this was through education and cultural transformation. In fact, he wrote numerous essays and novels that advocated for the enlightenment of the Filipino people and the development of national consciousness.

Despite the circumstances surrounding his family's ejection from their hacienda, he devoted his life to the betterment of his countrymen and worked tirelessly to expose the injustices during the Spanish times. His legacy lives on today, as he is widely regarded as the Philippines' national hero and his ideas continue to inspire generations of Filipinos.

A meticulously crafted replica of the Rizal mansion in Calamba, Laguna has been erected on the same site as the original structure, now standing as a national shrine and an important cultural landmark.

The story of Rizal's ejection from Calamba is a complex and nuanced one that sheds light on the challenges faced by Filipinos during the colonial period. While it may be uncomfortable to confront the realities of this chapter in our history, it is important to do so in order to gain a more complete understanding of our past and the struggles of those who fought for our freedom and independence.

It is important to remember that history is often written by the victors, and the official narrative may not always reflect the truth. In the case of Rizal's eviction from Calamba, it is clear that the story has been carefully curated to promote a certain narrative. However, it is only by examining the full story that we can gain a deeper understanding of the past and the complex forces that shaped it.

These administration buildings were responsible for the management of the Hacienda de Calamba.

CHAPTER XII
THE DAMAGING 'INGLISERO' CULTURE

The use of ethnic slurs in the Philippines is a topic that is often swept under the rug, yet it is a pervasive issue that plagues the country's cultural fabric. Members of the indio principalía, especially those who have spent time in the United States and returned as balikbayans, are notorious for coining slurs. Despite their limited English proficiency, they have managed to create pejoratives that have been widely adopted, such as Kastilaloy, Chinóy (Tsinoy), and Pinoy.

However, these words have deep-seated and racist connotations that we have unfortunately normalized without much thought. For example, Kastilaloy refers to an offspring of a Spaniard and a monkey (ung-góy), and Pinoy has been revealed to be just as profoundly offensive. Yet, the media, in its ignorance, has legitimized the use of Pinoy (an offspring of a Filipino and an ung-góy), perpetuating its harmful effects.

The emergence of the "inglisero" and "inglisera" syndrome, which is closely related to the coining of ethnic slurs, is a cultural trend where individuals rely heavily on English, even when speaking with others who are more comfortable with Tagalog or the local language. This behavior often includes a condescending attitude toward those who do not possess the same level of English proficiency, resulting in a snobbish class of people that looks down upon fellow citizens for not being able to speak English fluently.

The lack of English proficiency among our students and citizens has not gone unnoticed, with the International Monetary Fund attributing this problem to the Department of Education's "traditional inefficiency" dating back to the 1925 Monroe Commission on Philippine-American education. The compulsory teaching of English has resulted in the emergence of the inglisero and inglisera class, who exhibit an elitist syndrome that stems from their ignorance and intolerance of Spanish and other native languages.

According to some prominent figures in Philippine history, the emergence of derogatory terms can be traced back to a loss of national identity. Senator Claro M. Recto and National Artist for Literature Nick Joaquín attributed this loss to the compulsory shift from Spanish to English that the Americans mandated during their colonial rule. Recto argued that the forced adoption of English, which replaced Spanish and native languages in schools and other aspects of social life, created a rupture in cultural continuity within clans.

Unfortunately, this social fissure has largely gone unnoticed, as the struggling middle class is more preoccupied with their daily survival than with how the national language policy has negatively impacted learning. Although the harmful

According to Senator Claro M. Recto, the "inglisero syndrome" is silently causing a disruption in our society's cultural continuity. This YouTube video exemplifies an awkward situation where language serves as a barrier between a child and her father.

effects of this "violent change" may be gradual, they can accumulate and ultimately become a cancerous threat to the country's economic health. To prevent this from happening, it is important to examine the impact of language policies on a diverse country like the Philippines, with its many languages, ethnicities, and historical experiences.

To prevent this social issue from escalating further, we must review our history to understand how we have come to this point and find solutions to the problem. We need to examine the impact of the American invasion and economic colonialism, which insisted that English be the medium of instruction in our education system. We must also consider the veracity of our "national revolution against Spain" and how it has affected our country, which is comprised of various languages, ethnicities, and historical experiences.

Moreover, we need to recognize the importance of protecting our native languages outside of Tagalog, as tokenism is not enough to ensure their preservation. Unfortunately, education policymakers and politicians are often tone-deaf when it comes to fostering culture and native languages, resulting in the death of local literature and culture. It is a sad reality that in Iloilo City, there is hardly any daily newspaper in Ylongo or Hiligaynon, leading to the demise of their literature.

As Pope Francis visits the University of Santo Tomás, someone in the crowd expresses trenchant disapproval upon learning that the Pope will address them in Spanish.

As a society, we must address these issues and work toward preserving our cultural heritage and linguistic diversity. It is only by acknowledging our past mistakes that we can pave the way for a better future for all Filipinos.

※

IN 2015, DURING a visit from His Holiness Pope Francis to the campus of the University of Santo Tomás, a disconcerting display of linguistic intolerance occurred. As the emcee announced that the Pope would address the gathering in his mother tongue, Spanish, a vehement objection was unexpectedly heard across the campus. It is indeed lamentable that the Pontiff, a Spanish speaker, was subjected to hostility for using his own language. This incident left many audience members feeling shocked and embarrassed.

This occurrence is a regrettable example of the bigotry shown by certain individuals in the Philippines toward the Spanish language. The Philippines, a country where Spanish has played a significant role for over three centuries, has witnessed such fanaticism on other occasions. This type of intolerance stems from the rigid "English only" education system and the purist attitude toward language. It is important, however, to remember the rich cultural heritage that exists in the Filipino-Spanish community as a result of this history.

Despite the provision of simultaneous interpretation in English, the objection to Spanish was disruptive. This shameful incident serves as a reminder that Hispanophobia, the blind hatred for Spanish and the cultures it represents, is still present in the Philippines.

※

IT'S A HEARTBREAKING truth that in today's world, the real executioners of Rizal are the ingliseros. These individuals have been miseducated, even in Philippine history, and are grossly misled by the purista "culture." Rizal, who dreamed of a tolerant country, one that was confident in its ability to mingle with other nations and proud of its history and culture, would be disheartened by this state of affairs.

Rizal was known as a polyglot because of his passion for soaking up the culture of every country he visited, especially Spain, where he spoke the language. Sadly, the same country for which he sacrificed his life is now helping to extinguish his legacy through the actions of the Tagalog puristas. By removing the Spanish language from school curricula, they are depriving their compatriots of the real history of their country. It is a tragedy because some of the greatest literary treasures of the Philippines were written in Spanish.

The Tagalog puristas are responsible for perpetuating an educational system that creates social inequities through a bastardized form of "Pilipino chauvinism." This form of patriotism is being propagated as an educated one, but in reality, it is coarsely deficient and twisted. It lacks dignity and serves only the elite, while the rest of the country suffers the consequences.

It is time to recognize the importance of preserving the Spanish language and culture in the Philippines. Let us honor Rizal's legacy by embracing our country's diverse history and promoting the education of our citizens in all aspects of our shared heritage. Only then can we achieve the dream of a truly tolerant and progressive Philippines.

CHAPTER XIII
INVENTED LANGUAGE IS RUINING OUR CULTURE

It's hard to argue with the thesis that the eradication of a language is tantamount to the destruction of the culture that language embodies. A dead tongue represents a dead civilization. But, what defines a dead language? According to a United Nations agency, there are two definitions: First, language is dead when it's no longer spoken by any existing community. Examples include old Latin and old Greek. Second, a language is dead when it's no longer used as a development tool by a community that still speaks it.

The Ylongo or Hiligaynon language in the Philippines is an example of this. Though a large community still speaks it, it's no longer used as a tool for development, has no written media, and is no longer an official language in the community where it's spoken. Hiligaynon is running out of time since no books are regularly written or published in this language, making it a language on the verge of extinction.

Ermita Chavacano is another example of a dead vernacular in the Philippines. No one in Ermita, Manila, speaks it anymore. Another language that's fast disappearing in its cradle is Cavite Chavacano. Unfortunately, the Cavite City government seems to have no official program to save it.

Confined to a small seashore barangay (village), the few remaining speakers of Cavite Chavacano complain of ongoing cultural destruction due to official neglect. On the other hand, the Zamboanga City government deserves commendation for its active pro-Chavacano language programs. Zamboanga Chavacano has even grabbed the attention of foreign visitors who flock to Zamboanga to hear the native speakers and to learn the only existing Spanish-Latin Creole in Asia.

As it is, Spanish itself can also be considered a dead language in the Philippines since its official status was abolished by the 1987 Cory Constitution due to political expediency and Hispanophobia. The framers of the constitution gave up what could have been a significant advantage for the country in the age of globalization. Spanish is a world language spoken by over half a billion people globally, making it the second most widely spoken language after Chinese Mandarin in terms of native speakers.

Interestingly, Spanish is widely spoken in the United States, giving rise to a new generation of mainstream Americans embracing Latino artists like Jennifer López and Shakira. Meanwhile, in the Philippines, the government's overemphasis on English as the only official language of the country has converted Tagalog-based Filipino and ten other Philippine regional languages into dead lan-

Members of the Committee on National Language of the 1971 Philippine Constitutional Convention hold a public hearing to decide on the country's national language. After much deliberation, they eventually voted to adopt Filipino, not Pilipino, as the official language of the Philippines.

guages. The reason is that none of them, including Filipino itself, is being used as a tool of development in their respective communities of origin.

Isaac Donoso, a professor at the University of Valencia and an expert on Philippine literature in Spanish, describes this situation as a pernicious "diglossia," where the government zealously protects one language (English) at the expense of the other existing languages of the country.

The diglossia obtaining in the Philippines is prevalent due to the Katipunan purista culture and false "nationalism." As an old Ylongo composo points out: "Ining bag-ong pagtulun-an tama guid kasabad, babae, lalake nagakuyaw-kuyaw, kon sila maghambal puro guid ininglis gali kon sayuron, kay enamores...If I will go, sa hagdan makadto, gali kun sayuron si Inday malagyo..."

※

THE ISSUE OF the increasing illiteracy rate among Filipino students is currently being examined with a critical eye. There are inquiries being made regarding the root cause of this problem, such as the questions of how, who, when, and why this situation started to occur. Throughout the pages of this publication, the real culprit behind this national calamity is identified as the "contra vida." This personage is none other than Dean C. Worcester (October 1, 1866–May 2, 1924), a significant member of the colonial Philippine Commission, which was established by the victorious Americans as a legislative body with limited executive powers to aid in the governance of the nation shortly after their invasion in 1899.

The Philippine Organic Act, which was passed by the U.S. Congress in 1902, institutionalized the commission's legislative and executive powers. Worcester was also one of the leading members of the bicameral legislature established in 1907. At some point in his career, Worcester served as the Philippine interior secretary. He was an ardent supporter of American imperialism, who conducted controversial studies of the Igorots that many Filipinos considered racist.

On January 23, 1909, while still serving as interior secretary, he filed a libel suit against *El Renacimiento*, a pro-independence newspaper, for publishing an editorial entitled "Aves de rapiña" (Birds of Prey) on October 30 of the previous year. The scathing editorial referred to Worcester as "the eagle," the "most rapacious" bird of prey, and severely criticized American authorities "who, besides being eagles, have the characteristics of the vulture, the owl, and the vampire."

Worcester alleged that the newspaper had crossed the line when it accused certain American officials of using their racial studies of the Igorots as a cover for a more sinister aim, which was to enrich themselves by prospecting for gold in Northern Luzon. The suit was described as a landmark case during the U.S. colonial period by University of the Philippines Professor Luis V. Teodoro in an article in *The Daily Guardian* (February 26, 2014).

> Although the paper did not name him, Worcester filed a libel suit which resulted in the conviction of Fidel Reyes, who wrote the editorial, his co-editor Teodoro M. Kalaw, and publisher Martin Ocampo. Kalaw and Ocampo appealed the decision before the Philippine Supreme Court and later, the U.S. Supreme Court, but their conviction was affirmed in both. Although pardoned by then U.S. Governor-General Francis Burton Harrison in 1914, Ocampo had to pay the then huge amount of ₱100,000 in fines, which so crippled the paper and its sister newspaper *Muling Pagsilang* [edited by Lope K. Santos] both ceased publication.

Kalaw and Reyes made a veiled reference to Worcester as "un ave de rapiña" or a bird of prey. However, Don Napoleon Rama, a well-known Cebuano patriot and publisher of the Cebu daily *La Nueva Fuerza* with a Cebuano language section called "Bag-ong Kusog," did not mince words. He identified the American official as "ang Americanhon nga labing kaaway kang mga Filipinhon" or the worst enemy of the Filipino people. Let us recall the words written in Cebuano by the hispanista Napoleon Rama in 1915.

> Sa mga dagkung ciudad sa Estados Unidos siya naguihatag ng mga conferencia diin guinapaniguro niya nga kitang mga Filipinhon dili angay tagaan sa

kaugalingnan (independencia) kay pulos pa kita mga gunggung. Ug aron sa pamatuod sa iyang mga pulong, guipakita niya pinaagui sa mga sintas sa cine ang mga Igorrote nga naghubo (nga ang uban kuno nagakaon iro) ug silingon niya nga kini ang mga pumuluyo sa Filipinas. Tuod man. Ang libo ka libo ka mga Americanhon nga namati kaniya nanoo dayon nga ang nga Filipinhon salvaje ug busa dili angay tagaan sa kaugalingnan.

The accounts of notable Spanish-speaking Filipinos, including Rama, regarding the disgraceful position of Worcester in our past, should be adequate. If Worcester is not recognized by the English-speaking Filipinos today, it is because in the retelling of our history, the role of the villain is attributed to Rizal's fictional friar, Padre Dámaso, and not to the actual villain, Worcester. The malignant part he played in our history has been kept concealed from scrutiny.

※

THE AMERICAN COLONIZERS had a clear objective when it came to education and culture in the Philippines, and that was to remove the Spanish language from the national identity and replace it with English. This goal aligned with President William McKinley's instructions to "Christianize," "civilize," and "uplift" the Filipino people, effectively turning them into a labor force that the Americans could exploit. Despite Spanish being a medium of instruction since the Spanish educational reforms of 1863, Worcester was determined to get rid of it.

To achieve this goal, Worcester needed the cooperation of Katipunan Abakada puristas like Lope K. Santos, who worked with the Thomasite teachers. However, their primary objective was not to educate Filipino children but to remove Spanish and replace it with English. If they had only focused on adding English to the curriculum instead of replacing Spanish, Philippine education could have been superior. Their efforts to prevent Filipinos from using Spanish slowed down the educational process. Worcester's collaborators, like Santos, introduced purista Abakada Tagalog as a compulsory subject. Santos wrote an intricate Abakada purista Tagalog grammar book called Balarila, along with an alphabet known as Abakada. Abakada consisted of only twenty letters and replaced the Tagalog catón, which featured the Spanish alphabet (Abecedario) of thirty-two letters, which Filipinos had used since at least 1610.

Worcester met Santos, also a Katipunan Mason, because he had sued him for libel for writing the Tagalog version of "Aves de rapiña," translated as "Mga ibong mandaraguit." However, Santos was acquitted, and Worcester soon offered him an olive branch by hiring him to implement his plan to de-Hispanize Tagalog. Their partnership reduced Tagalog into a backward pre-Hispanic language that lacked modern letters like C, F, J, LL, Ñ, Q, V, and Z. They removed these letters from Tagalog supposedly to eliminate Spanish vocabulary that had seeped into the language over three centuries. They resorted to inventing new words that sounded so artificial and ridiculous that even the Tagalog themselves refused to use them. An example of these words is salumpuwit, which never replaced silla in Tagalog.

Tomás Pinpin, a chino cristiano printer, was the most prominent user of the Abecedario. He was the first Filipino to publish a book in the Philippines, with his *Librong Pagaaralan nang mga Tagalog nang Uicang Castilla* (Reference Book for Learning Castellano in Tagalog). He produced his book in two versions, one in Tagalog to help his fellow citizens learn Spanish quickly and the other in Chinese. A Spanish grammar book he authored featured the Abecedario, which Tagalog writers like Francisco Balagtas extensively used to compose their awit, including the Tagalog classic *Florante at Laura*.

In the 1970s, the practice of coining Tagalog words was stopped. However, the imposition of the Abakada in national language classes had a negative impact on students' attitude toward the Tagalog language. They associate the Abakada with some aspects of Philippine pre-Hispanic culture, which is considered flawed by puristas because it supposedly cannot articulate the fricative sound of F.

It is a fabrication to say that nobody in the Philippines can articulate the sound of the letter F, much less write it. Some vernaculars have the F sound, such as the Igorot vernacular, where the word for rice is inafi. Some Lumads in Mindanao have names like Mac-Falen.

Because of the unfounded No-F disinformation, puristas found it easier to obtain policymakers' imprimatur for changing F to P in Filipino and Filipinas. This made us a laughing stock of other countries, which have always known us as Filipinos and our country as Filipinas.

Dean C. Worcester is photographed with a person whom he described as a "representative Negrito man," a significant subject of his ethnographic research.

Virgilio Almario, former head of the National Commission for Culture and the Arts and the Komisyon sa Wikang Filipino, proposed to correct this error since the present constitution already provides the official name of our national language as Filipino, not Pilipino. The Committee on National Language of the 1971 Philippine Constitutional Convention voted to adopt Filipino, not Pilipino, as the country's national language. However, Almario's efforts were frustrated by ignorant elements in Congress who complained about the financial cost of changing signages and printing new official stationeries.

The Abakada has been replaced by an Anglicized Filipino alphabet, including the letter F, which was removed for no valid linguistic and cultural reasons except to satisfy the Worcester-Santos tandem in their insane social experiment to foment a false indigenous nationalism out of hatred for our Spanish heritage.

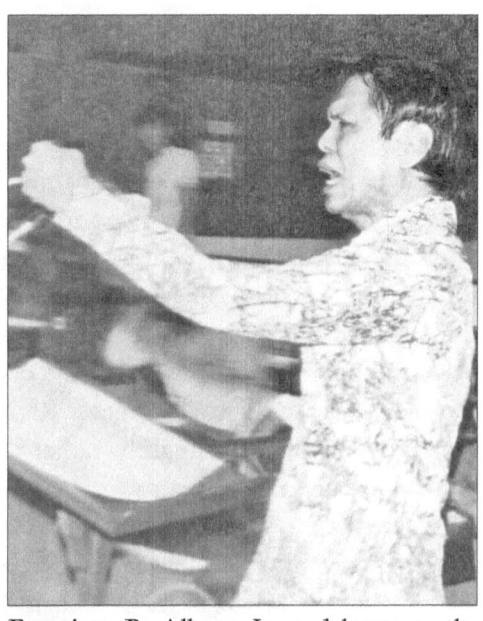

Francisco B. Albano Jr., a delegate to the 1971 Constitutional Convention from Isabela, gives a spirited speech during a debate on the national language.

WE ARE ENCOURAGED by the fact that the Iloilo *Sumakwelan*, an important resource for the teaching of Hiligaynon, has not been swayed by the outdated and unpopular Tagalog Abakada purista ideology. In fact, the proposed letters of the Hiligaynon alphabet by *Sumakwelan* still maintain almost the same pronunciation as the old Abecedario: A, Be, De, E, Ele, Eme, Ene, and so on. However, *Sumakwelan* should take a further step by reintroducing all the letters that were discarded with the introduction of the Abakada, such as C and F.

In the *Fundamental Principles of the Hiligaynon Language* (Iloilo 2009), *Sumakwelan* explains that the current Ylongo alphabet consists of the following letters: A, Be, K, De, E, Ge, He, I, He, eLe, eMe, eNe, O, Pe, eSe, Te, U, We, and Ye. In comparison, the now outdated Abakada only includes the following letters: A, ba, Ka, Da, E, Ga, Ha, I, La, Ma, Na, Ng, O, Pa, Ra, Sa, Ta, U, Wa, and Ya.

Sumakwelan aims to preserve the Ylongo language by teaching that consonants in the Hiligaynon alphabet should be pronounced with the phoneme E instead of the phoneme A, which is promoted by the Abakada.

The Komisyon sa Wikang Filipino has adhered to the constitution by adopting an English-influenced thirty-one letter alphabet, which includes the letter Ñ. *Sumakwelan* should also integrate the letters C, F, J, Ñ, LL, Q, V, and Z into its Hiligaynon alphabet.

IN PREVIOUS CHAPTERS of this work, we have expounded upon the deleterious effects of neologisms in Tagalog on the learning capabilities of our young scholars. While this linguistic issue may be somewhat intricate, we shall, at the risk of redundancy, delve further into it and provide additional illustrations.

After more than a century of adherence to the Worcester-Santos agenda, illiteracy has become rampant among our students, prompting the World Bank and the International Monetary Fund to sound the alarm. The escalating illiteracy plaguing our public schools is not the current Department of Education's fault as it was not an overnight occurrence. Rather, the haphazard American initiative of replacing Spanish with English, rather than supplementing English to the educational curriculum, is to blame.

As we have previously noted, the Abakada—a twenty-letter alphabet—proved inferior to the Spanish alphabet of thirty-two letters that had already been introduced to our native languages by Tomás Pinpin in 1611 and utilized in literature by Balagtas when he composed his classic awit, *Florante at Laura*, in 1838.

Regrettably, Worcester's agenda, utilizing the Abakada as his primary weapon, has left our children lagging in education. They have wasted invaluable time in classrooms respelling and resyllabicating Spanish words that had already been an integral part of our everyday native vocabulary, including Dios to Diyos; Filipinas to Pilipinas; Cristo to Kristo; escuela to iskwilahan; cine to sine; chinelas to tsinelas; and Chino to Tsino, and so forth.

After a century of this practice, yielding no discernible gains, we must ask ourselves: what have we achieved as a people in language and culture by changing Dios to Diyos and Filipinas to Pilipinas?

Moreover, in addition to expending time and effort in respelling and resyllabicating thousands of Spanish words, our public schoolteachers and their students were compelled to learn thousands of fabricated words such as Balarila, pandiwa, pang angkop, pang halip, and sugnay at parirala, among others, to replace their Spanish equivalents in Tagalog and other major native languages. These Spanish words, such as gramática, verbo, adjetivo, pronombre, and subjeto y predicado, had already been adopted as Tagalog words and were used in old textbooks to teach all the native languages.

Numerous teachers and school administrators have voiced their concern about elementary pupils dropping out because they struggled with learning an almost entirely new language that Santos had invented. Had he and Worcester not meddled with our educational system, learning would have been more accessible since many Spanish words have obvious cognates in their English language equivalents.

Yet, in his distorted sense of colonial wisdom, Worcester commissioned Santos to devise neologisms for the teachers to learn before teaching the newly coined words to their students. This resulted in a hybrid language that only Santos and his so-called team of experts could understand. This process of de-Hispanization of language has inflicted damage upon the intellectual, educational, cultural, and technical training of our people.

Our leaders must awaken and remedy the significant harm that has been wrought upon our educational system. A substantial part of the solution is to restore the Spanish Abecedario, along with the language and culture it represents, while preserving the few positive developments of present trends. However, does the government listen? Will the government act?

What tangible advancements have we made in language and culture by changing "Filipinas" to "Pilipinas"?

CHAPTER XIV
THE INTELLECTUAL DEFICIENCY OF PURISTAS

The issue of language and culture in the Philippines has been a subject of debate for many years, with various groups advocating for the preservation and development of the country's rich linguistic and cultural heritage. One of the most controversial aspects of this debate is the role of the Tagalog Abakada puristas, a minority group that has been accused of undermining the natural evolution of the Tagalog language and the broader Filipino national identity.

Despite their small numbers, the Tagalog Abakada puristas have been able to exert significant influence on the country's educational system, thanks to their capture of government power. This has enabled them to institutionalize their Abakada purista culture, particularly in the teaching of the so-called national language subjects. Through this process, they have been able to impose their twenty-letter Abakada and their invented spelling system upon generations of Filipino schoolchildren.

The roots of this controversy can be traced back to the Commonwealth era when President Manuel L. Quezon signed an executive order in 1937 declaring Tagalog as the basis of an aspirational national language. At that time, Lope K. Santos, the inventor of Abakada and Tagalog grammar called Balarila became the default source for teaching the national language.

However, Santos' mania for neologism came with his re-imagined lexicon that has damaged the natural evolution of Tagalog as the basis of the national language project.

One particularly interesting anecdote related to the controversy surrounding the Tagalog Abakada puristas is that of President Quezon throwing Santos' Balarila grammar book into the Pasig River. This incident reportedly occurred because even Quezon, a native Tagalog speaker, could not, as told by the late Senator Soc Rodrigo, understand the content of the book. This story serves to highlight the absurdity of the Abakada puristas' insistence on their twenty-letter alphabet and their invented spelling system, which even the president of the Philippines found incomprehensible.

However, despite Quezon's personal distaste for the Abakada-Balarila culture, it was still able to gain a foothold in the country's educational system due to the strong support it received from the U.S. colonizers of that era. This anecdote serves as a reminder of the complex history and politics surrounding language and culture in the Philippines, and the ways in which seemingly minor decisions can have long-lasting and far-reaching consequences.

Lope K. Santos

Santos' Abakada of only twenty letters effectively replaced the 1610 Tomás Pinpin Abecedario of thirty-two letters, which had been encrusted into all our native languages through the Spanish introduction of the printing press. This had resulted in classic Tagalog writers and poets like Francisco Balagtas using Pinpin's Spanish Abecedario to compose their obras maestras, most notably the immortal epic *Florante at Laura*.

However, the Abakada puristas of the 1960s argued against the Spanish spelling of this Tagalog masterpiece, insisting that it should be spelled as "Plorante at Laura." This spelling change caused controversy among many, including the late University of the Philippines history professor and author Teodoro A. Agoncillo, who embraced the thinking of the Tagalog Abakada puristas and even wrote an article justifying this spelling change.

Upon hearing Agoncillo's convoluted argument and semantic nonsense that strained credulity, Tio Emilio Severino, a Hiligaynon poet and Spanish writer from Silay, Negros Occidental, expressed complete shock and disbelief, stating "Agoncillo must have gone mad. Está loco."

All in all, the controversy surrounding the Tagalog Abakada puristas highlights the importance of preserving and developing the Philippines' linguistic and cultural heritage while also recognizing the natural evolution of these languages. It also underscores the need for informed and thoughtful debate around issues of language and culture in the country.

※

IN THE 1970S, Severino was at the helm of the Katilingban sang Madia-as, a Visayan Ylongo language group that presented itself before the National Language Committee of the 1971-73 Constitutional Convention. Along with the Lubas sa Dagang Bisaya of Cebu, led by Natalio Bacalso, they voiced their opposition to the mandatory teaching of Tagalog and the use of Santos' purist Abakada-Balarila as a textbook. Bacalso was a well-known radio journalist and film producer from Cebu, best known for his film, *Mutya sa Saguing Tindok*.

Simply put, a long-simmering language issue was brought to a boil by an obstinate and conniving Tagalog Abakada-Balarila purist clique who, like parasites, have exploited our educational system for their own gain, profiting off the

backs of our students. They created an artificial situation that inundated the national government's largest bureaucracy, the Department of Education, in Abakada-Balarila culture, affording themselves a boundless financial stream that sends them off chuckling to the bank. This situation calls to mind the U.S. military-industrial complex, which sees Iran, Afghanistan, China, Russia, or some other bogeymen as "enemies" of the United States, thereby creating instability throughout the world and fueling forever wars to sell their weapons.

In our case, an education mafia exists. And they are imposing their Abakada-Balarila textbooks on all non-Tagalog-speaking students, revising the spellings of thousands of Spanish words already familiar to non-Tagalogs through their native languages and replacing them with ridiculous made-up words like salumpuwit for silla. By expunging Spanish words from the Tagalog language and replacing them with nonsensical language, the purists have succeeded in making the same Tagalog-based national language subject a difficult and bothersome subject to teach and learn for generations.

With perennial budget shortfalls and endemic corruption in government, our students and teachers have been subjected to overcrowded classrooms of up to fifty or more students. As if it weren't bad enough to have large classes taught by underpaid and poorly trained teachers and attended by many underprivileged students, they also had to endure the added misery of an almost incomprehensible Abakada-Balarila Tagalog subject. One can only imagine the challenges they faced during the Covid-19 pandemic with an exceedingly inadequate remote learning module.

The Tagalog Abakada purist mafia has entrenched itself in the educational system, and it will continue to do so until government officials realize the harmful effects of Abakada culture as the primary cause of functional illiteracy. This affliction plagues eighty percent of Filipino students across all levels of education, as revealed by the PISA survey and the IMF-World Bank.

The Philippines first participated in the PISA survey in 2018, finishing last among seventy-nine "participating countries and economies in reading and second to last in science and mathematics," according to the organization. The 2020 PISA survey results were even more damning but not surprising to those who have long diagnosed the source of this problem:

> The overwhelming majority of students in the Philippines failed to reach minimum levels of proficiency across all three PISA subjects, with a wide gap by socioeconomic status. *About 81 percent of students scored below minimum proficiency levels in reading and math, and 78 percent in science* (underscoring ours). These challenges in foundational skills start at early grades: a significant proportion of students do not demonstrate that they understand what they are reading in English by the end of Grade 3 (Education Development Center 2018). This weak proficiency in English severely constrains the learning ability of students in all subjects in later grades. Performance varied by sociodemographic characteristics, such as gender (in favor of girls), school ownership (in favor of students in private independent schools), and socioeconomic status (in favor of socioeconomically advantaged students). The high level of social segregation in the Philippines—a typical disadvantaged student has about a one-in-seven chance of attending the same school as high-achieving peers—seemed to reinforce performance gaps.

Suppose the movement to amend the constitution to grant autonomy to the regions succeeds, Tagalog-Pilipino is likely to decrease in non-Tagalog areas. This is due to the increasing use of several pidgins like Taglish and Cebuglish. The decline of Tagalog-Pilipino is the outcome of the Tagalog Abakada puristas' advocacy against the original Hispanic identity of all Filipinos. Their behavior can be traced back to the creation of an incomprehensible language at the behest of American colonialists like Dean C. Worcester, who played a significant role in the early days of U.S. colonization in the early 1900s.

Don Napoleon Rama, a respected Cebuano writer who wrote for the defunct daily, *La Nueva Fuerza-Bag-ong Kusog*, labeled Worcester as the greatest enemy of the Filipino people. The Tagalog Abakada puristas engendered by Lope K. Santos, who perpetrate his dysfunctional system, are a hindrance to national progress due to the foreign provenance of this cancer that continues to gnaw at our educational system.

By and large, the Tagalog Abakada puristas are a hindrance to our native languages. They are inferior to intellectual giants like Teodoro M. Kalaw and Claro M. Recto, both Tagalog men of letters, and Spanish-speaking Visayans who have also mastered their native tongues like Delfín Gumbán and Flavio Zaragoza Cano, Don Napoleon Rama, Antonio Abád, Manuel Briones, and José del Mar, among many other patriots.

IF YLONGOS WERE to have a federal system like the Muslims, they could potentially become an economically self-sufficient state. The Bangsamoro Autonomous Region in Muslim Mindanao, on the other hand, was hastily created and constitutionally weak, requiring an annual budget of eighty billion pesos to support its economically unproductive yet heavily armed members from reported Malaysian-sponsored Muslim groups.

Unlike the Catholic Ylongos, some Muslims believe that Christians, being "gentiles," have a duty to support them for life. This ideology drove them to piracy as their primary economic source during the Spanish regime. They would often raid the Christian provinces of Iloilo, Negros, and Cebu, stealing their rice, corn, women, and young boys. The rice and corn were for their consumption, as agriculture was almost foreign to them, while the women and young boys were enslaved or sold to markets in Southeast Asia.

The Spanish administration put an end to these piratical practices, but not without prolonged conflict that lasted for two hundred years, known as the "Moro Wars." They built seaside fortresses and churches with bell towers, like that of Miag-ao, Iloilo, and Bohol, which doubled as fortresses of resistance and refuge for the townspeople. The Spanish government imported steamships with cannons to overtake and sink the fast and massive Muslim pirate vintas. Despite this history, some revisionists glorify the Muslims for their resistance to Spanish colonization, even though they raided and confiscated the rice harvests of non-Muslim regions. The Ilocanos, for instance, still preserve anti-pirate stone towers in old Namacpacan (now Luna) in La Union, along with beautiful stone seashore fortifications in Vigan and Laoag.

These piratical "traditions" have been replaced with an annual eighty billion-peso subsidy from mostly Christian taxpayers, supporting the Bangsamoro Autonomous Region in Muslim Mindanao.

Ylongos have managed to maintain economic stability without resorting to violent extortion due to their legacy of producing goods such as sugar, rice, abaca, corn, coffee, cacao, and coconuts, as well as maintaining vegetable granjas. The preservation of their old Spanish traditions such as amor propio, delicadeza, dignidad, and palabra de honor has resulted in visible progress in provinces like Iloilo and other parts of Western Visayas.

THE INDEPENDENT HISTORY OF YLONGO AND CEBUANO VISAYANS

Spanish fortifications scattered throughout the archipelago protected against Moro pirate raids. 1. Fuerte de San Vicente Ferrer, Maribojoc, Bohol 2. Fuerza de Sta. Isabel, Taytay, Palawan 3. Guimbal watchtowers, Guimbal, Iloilo 4. Real de Fuerte de Nuestra Señora del Pilar de Zaragoza, Zamboanga City 5. Twin Forts of Romblon, Romblon 6. Fuerte de San Vicente Ferrer, Maribojoc, Bohol 7. Oslob watchtower, Oslob, Cebu 8. Fort Santiago, Intramuros, Manila.

CHAPTER XV
THE RACE TO PROTECT YLONGO IDENTITY

Identity is a complex and multi-faceted concept that involves a multitude of factors, including one's name, ethnicity, culture, language, and food preferences. In the Philippines, identity hinges on two critical elements: the name one answers to and the primary staple food and cooking style that defines one's cuisine. It is fascinating to explore the nuances of these factors that make up the unique Filipino identity, especially in the context of the ongoing debate over language and cultural preservation.

When it comes to names of places and surnames of individuals and persons, many people mistakenly believe that they should be spelled and pronounced according to the new Abakada invention. However, this is not the case. In reality, these names are in Spanish or spelled and pronounced according to the old Spanish Abecedario. For instance, Tagalog surnames like Dimaculañgan, Manguiat, Dimaguiba, Campi, and Maglaque are not abakadized. Similarly, names of places such as Meicaoaian, Taguig, or Guiguinto follow the old Spanish pronunciation rules. Old documents show that it was also Cálao, not Kalaw, and Catigbác, not Katigbak.

Unfortunately, the new functional illiterates today join "de" and "la" or "de" and "los" to produce what is mistaken today as middle names like "Dela" and "Delos." This confusion leads to errors in surnames such as "De la Cruz," "De la Rosa," and "De los Santos" or "De los Reyes." Even our Chinese-derived surnames are Hispanized and not foolishly abakadized, including Locsin, Lacson, Ynciong, Gantuanco, Tantoco, Tantianco, Cajúcom, Tuáson, Quézon, Tanjutco, Litiatco, Lauchengco, Cojuangco, Diching, Limtuaco, Uichanco, Zaico, Súnico, and others.

The fundamental violation, however, is the replacement of F for P in Filipinas and Filipino, aside from bastardizing the title of the Balagtas masterpiece into "Plorante at Lawra." These are the inutile consequences, or traces, of the unnecessary Abakada purista trend foisted by U.S. colonialists like Worcester et al., followed by slavish locals influenced by the Masons. One such Mason was Trinidad Pardo de Tavera, a member of the 1902 Philippine Commission who authored a debunked history of the American census of 1905 and 1907.

Regarding nutrition, rice is the staple food of Ylongos, with the occasional morning pan de sal. Iloilo viand (dapli) is also the Hispanic tinola-puchero, the guisado, the inasal-asado, the pinirito-frito, the sinugba-parrilla, the lechón enjamonado, and the escabeche. Thus the Ylongo identity, like that of the other non-Tagalogs, is Spanish. However, the Hispanophobia of the Tagalog Abakada puristas threatens the Ylongo's individuality and harms the unifying Filipino identity of non-Tagalogs.

Since the American colonizers never controlled the Ylongo Voluntarios nor the Estado Federal de Visayas, these revisionisms in native appellations and names of places in the Visayas were spared from gross abakadization. Thus, the influence of backward abakadization in the Visayas, and even Mindanao, only came from Manila through the new educational system in English and Tagalog Abakada purista in the 1950s.

Abakadization has led to functional illiteracy, as international school surveys and random student tests have shown.

Replacing one-third of the letters in the thirty-two-letter Abecedario with the twenty-letter Abakada has undoubtedly contributed to the present state of functional and actual illiteracy plaguing the Filipino people.

In just one generation, the once flourishing Ylongo literature led by Delfín Gumbán, Flavio Zaragoza Cano, Magdalena Jalandoni, and Ramón L. Muzones declined until it began to decay and disappear. The crisis is classifying Ylongo as a dying language with almost non-existent publications today. Abakadization appears to be the main reason for its decay. Hiligaynon literature in print now resembles Tagalog purista garbage, lacking a reading market among Ylongo speakers and disappearing from street newsstands in greater Iloilo City, spelling the death of Hiligaynon literature. This situation also endangers the Ylongo Visayan identity and the identities of Cebuanos and Samar-Leyteños.

Given this overall situation, legislators and leaders must take action. Puristas have ruined quality education in the country, and we must protect our Spanish legacy and language. Many of our great erudite minds and patriots have pointed out that "without Spanish, the national identity of the Philippines will be truncated and destroyed."

CHAPTER XVI
EPIC REVEALS ADVANCED
PRE-HISPANIC CULTURE

The Tagalogs do not have a complete pre-Hispanic history like the Ylongos have in their *Maragtas* (annals). However, they do have a fragmented narrative called the *Kulintang-kumintang,* which may even be a lost chapter of the Ylongos' *Maragtas.*

On the other hand, the *Maragtas* is an oral history of the ten Bornean datus who arrived in San Joaquín town on Panay Island in the twelfth century. They came with their respective followers or sacopes, which consisted of around a hundred families per datu, aboard rigged boats called barangay or balangay. They left northern Borneo because their ruler, Rajah Macatunao, had wanted them killed, and one possibility for his anger toward them was due to religion.

It is speculated that the datus and their respective barangays preferred to remain animists and refused to convert to Islam. The refugees were led by Datu Puti, who was physically strong, handsome, and wise. Along with him came lawgivers like Datus Calanti-ao and Sumacuel, and even a woman lawgiver called Lubluban. They did not come to Panay as invaders, but rather as peaceful settlers.

In exchange for land to settle in Panay, they were said to have given gold and pearls to the aboriginal Aetas, led by King Maricudo and his wife, Queen Mani-uanti-uan. They subdivided Panay into several datuships under the Confederation of Madia-as. Panay Island was then called Aninipay. Madia-as is located

The "Maragtas" epic recounts the perilous journey of ten Bornean datus and their followers who fled their homeland in search of refuge from tyranny. To escape, they embarked on a treacherous voyage across the sea aboard makeshift boats called balangays or barangays.

in a mountain range near the island's center, next to a magical mountain called Bulalacao, connecting to a corollary mountain range.

※

AROUND 1853, FRAY Tomás Santarén, OSA took on the task of transcribing the *Maragtas* from its original language Ylongo-Quinaray-a. He then translated it into Spanish. Later on, a number of Ylongo writers, such as Pedro Alcantara Monteclaro in 1907, made modifications to the original Santarén manuscript to create a modern version in Hiligaynon. Delfín Gumbán, known as the "King of Ylongo Poetry," from Pavía town, Iloilo, adapted *Maragtas* into Hiligaynon verse using the Spanish meter in the 1930s. He later produced a new adaptation in Spanish verse titled *Odisea Legendaria* in 1941, for which he was awarded the Premio Zóbel de literatura in 1980. *Oda or Odisea Legendaria* or *El Maragtás* was included in Gumbán's poetry book, *Flores de invierno*.

In the college Spanish textbook *La literatura filipina y su relación al nacionalismo filipino*, the author includes some of Gumbán's *Maragtas* verses ("La Confederación de Madia-as"), which can be read as follows:

> Datu Puti optaba por volver a Borneo
> A organizar la lucha en su ardiente deseo
> De librar a su patria del tirano rapaz.
> Una confederación al caudillaje digno
> De Sumacuel formóse; fue el simbólico signo
> De la nación en ciernes, estructurada en paz.
>
> Las provincias de Cápiz, Iloilo y Antique
> En triángulo forman el histórico dique
> De unidad de esta región gloriosa
> Sumacuel en Antique, Paiburong en Iloilo,
> Bangcaya en Aclan-Cápiz, son nudos de un hilo,
> El hilo de amor que une a todo Hiligaynón.

The Madia-as Confederation subdivided Aninipay (Panay) into three datuships, each with its own ruler. Sumacuel governed Antique, Paibúrong, Iloilo, Bangcaya, Aclan, and Cápiz.

The Bornean datus who settled in Iloilo demonstrated a strong sense of nationhood and unity, spreading out to other Visayan islands such as Cebu, Leyte, Samar, and even northern Mindanao. They established datuships and rajahships, which eventually evolved into barangays and later into Spanish barrios.

After establishing a Tagalog datuship in Taal and Balayan, Batangas, Datu Puti and his mga sacop or sacopes are believed to be the forebears of the Tagalog people. This explains the similarity between many old Tagalog words and Hiligaynon words, and why the progenitors of present-day Batangueños and all Tagalogs in Luzon trace their roots to them.

The fact that Tagalogs and Bicolanos have Hiligaynon roots also explains their lack of any purely Tagalog pre-Hispanic tradition or history, which their Ylongo forebears possessed abundantly.

Gumbán's *Maragtas* verses, written in Ylongo Spanish, provide clear evidence of the discovery of the Taal River in Batangas and the subsequent settlement of the area by immigrants led by Datus Puti, Dumangsil, and Balensuyela, as follows:

> Era de noche cuando desplegaron la vela
> Datu Puti, Dumangsil junto a Balensuyela
> En viaje de retorno a la Isla de Bornay
> Les arreciaba en contra un borrascoso viento
> Que enfuriaba las olas del liquid element
> Cuando dejaban las costas de Panay.

Pure coincidence led the three datus to discover Luzon. This stanza narrates Datu Puti's intention to go back to Borneo with some of his followers to overthrow Macatunao from his throne. Unfortunately, the habagat or strong monsoon winds prevented them from reaching their destination and instead, they were forced to sail northward to Luzon.

> Los tres datus marinos creyeron de provecho
> Visitar la isla grande que navegar derecho
> Por la ruta más corta al soplo boreal.
> Y asi lo hicieron luego, en larga travesía,
> hasta que una mañana de un despejado día
> divisaron un río que llamaron Taal.

The three datus and their followers stumbled upon the vast Taal River (Pansipit) that flowed toward the present-day Taal Lake, a large bay that housed an active volcano.

> Y, a la boca que al mar daba aquel gran río,
> Se acercaron en busca de algún manantial frío.
> Arribaron. Bajaron. Y todo estaba en flor.
> Encantados por el sitio, los Datus se quedaron

Despite some historians discrediting the "Maragtas" as a myth, the provincial government of Antique honors the ten Bornean datus who played a crucial role in the epic. To commemorate their contribution, the government commissioned artist John Alaban (pictured in the foreground) to create towering sculptures of the chiefs, which are permanently exhibited at the Malandog Esplanade in Hamtic town.

> Con todas sus familias. Puti y otros marcharon
> Dejando en Taal nuevo humano vigor.

Captivated by the place, the three datus disembarked and opted to remain with their families and followers, bringing about a fresh start for Taal. Nonetheless, Datu Puti departed, likely to retrieve additional supporters, with the intent of permanently settling in Taal, Batangas, after toppling the oppressive Rajah Macatunao in distant Borneo.

※

THERE IS NO pre-Hispanic history that can compare with the *Maragtas*. This epic beautifully lays out the story of several datus who spread out from Panay and settled and colonized other islands with the intent of forming an Austronesian ethnic nation. Despite their noble intentions, they failed to complete or achieve their goal because they suffered from geographic isolation. The scattered settlers, divided by virgin lands and rough seas, were cut off from one another by a lack of communication. This kind of isolation stunted their progress, resulting in a poorly developed agricultural economy.

To our knowledge, no study exists to compare the coming to Iloilo of the Bornean datus as peaceful settler-colonizers and the first arrival of the Bornean

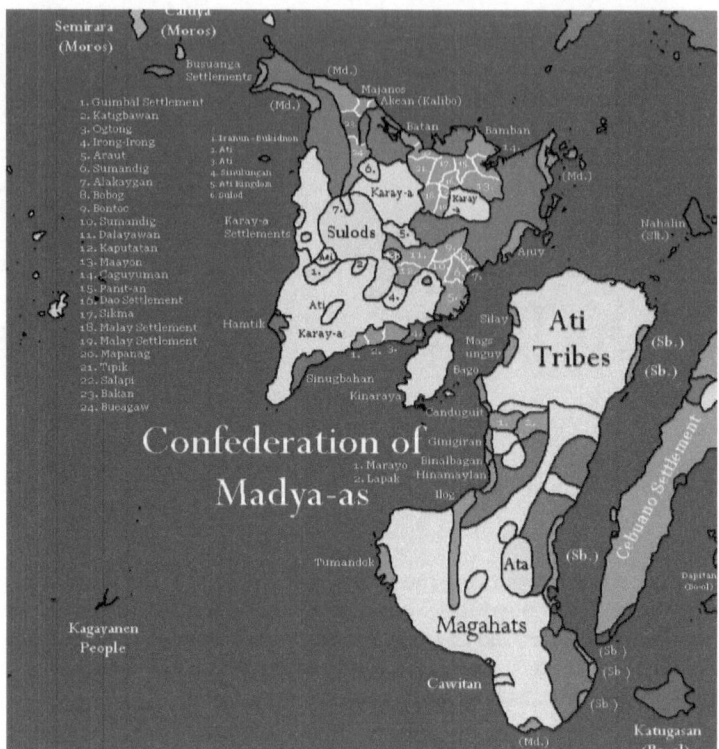

A map depicting the regions that made up the Confederation of Madia-as, alternatively spelled as Madya-as and Madja-as.

Moro missionaries to Mindanao in the thirteenth century. While the Moros came as semi-Islamic slave traders to subjugate the Lumad tribes of Maguindanao and Sulu, the Bornean datus did not take over the land by force but through negotiations that led to the famous Barter of Panay.

In Muslim Mindanao, the Lumads recall the story of two brothers born to royalty, Mamalu and Tabuwanay of Cotabato. The bloody violence that came with the arrival of the Moros destroyed their close relationship. Armed to the teeth, the Moros launched attacks on the Lumad tribes in Maguindanao and Sulu. They took Tabuwanay prisoner, along with his followers, and compelled them to convert to Islam under threat of death. His brother Mamalu and some of their followers fled to the mountain, and they were able to preserve their original culture and beliefs. The *Maragtas* marks and shows this difference in approach.

In the end, the Bornean datu settlers became Visayans who spread from Panay and Cebu to all over the other islands, including Mindanao. What the Spaniards later identified as Moros turned out to be a different and restless group that was always appeared at odds with all the others. In time, Visayans accepted the Spanish King as their sovereign, thereby becoming the Filipino nation with the Tagalogs, Pampangos, Ilocanos, and Bicolanos from Luzon as their authentic brothers. The Moros of Maguindanao and Sulu, however, became ethnographically different. Early editions of *Webster's* English language dictionary appeared to recognize this ethnographic difference, describing a Filipino (Sp.) as "a member of a Christianized Malayan tribe (or people), as distinguished from the pagan and wild tribes and the Mohammedan Moros."

The Bornean settlers relied on fishing for subsistence, but their hand-to-mouth existence was limited by their lack of agricultural technology, which forced them to resort to nomadic hunting and slash-and-burn farming in their new territory. They also lacked domesticated animals of burden like the carabao and the horse, which were only introduced later by Spanish friars and conquistadores.

The Spanish-Mexican galleons introduced new crops and farming methods, including corn, sugarcane, and better irrigation systems, as well as animals and staples like the carabao, guava, and coffee. Chinese migrants brought industry, business acumen, Chinese medicine, arts, and varied cuisines, including noodles that blended well with Spanish dishes.

However, the early Austronesian settlers did not develop lasting infrastructure, government culture, or an organized barter system.

The fragmentation of the common Austronesian language of the ten datus and their followers into several native dialects can be attributed to the spread of the legendary Austronesian datus from Panay. The introduction of Baybayin writing system for each dialect also contributed to the language's fragmentation, as these were mutually unintelligible. The need for a solid and uniting influence led to the Spanish language's introduction, which provided a more sophisticated idiom and strong cultural moorings.

The Spanish language enriched the native languages by introducing the Roman Abecedario and the basic Spanish phonemes of E and O, as well as additional consonants such as F, C, G, J, Ll, Ñ, Q, X, V, and Z. These refinements paved the way for the emergence of a new form of writing, the popular corrido-awit literature. The introduction of the printing press by Spanish friars and the influence of the Roman Catholic Church eventually led to the unification of the pre-Hispanic Ylongo *Maragtas* into one nation: El Pueblo Filipino.

CHAPTER XVII
VILLA DE ARÉVALO: ILOILO'S FIRST SPANISH PUEBLO

Villa de Arévalo, the first Spanish settlement in Iloilo, became a renowned shipbuilding center responsible for constructing galleon ships that sailed the Pacific Ocean between Manila and Acapulco for centuries. The Spanish conquistadores and missionaries, primarily Augustinians, Dominicans, and Jesuits, brought both indio Visayans and Chinese laborers to create a formidable workforce. The Chinese capataces, led by Spanish ship engineers, directed the indio laborers in producing galleons for trade, commerce, and national defense.

Besides the usual Moro piracy, Iloilo withstood numerous Dutch attacks from the Dutch East Indies, which we now know as Malaysia and Indonesia. Arévalo quickly grew and became a municipio, fueled by its shipbuilding industry, agriculture, livestock, food factories, and extensive weaving industries. The population grew with the influx of newcomers from other parts of Panay and the arrival of Chinese migrants. Many Chinese settlers entered into pre-arranged marriages with native Visayan women with the approval of the Augustinian Spanish friars. They were relocated to Molo to form a municipio and a sector de mestizos or a parián that also dealt in agriculture, weaving, fishing, and minor food industries.

The grand convent standing next to the Arévalo Catholic church is a testament to the district's historical significance as the pioneering Spanish settlement in Iloilo. As the birthplace of the modern metropolis, the area played a crucial role in shaping the region's cultural and economic landscape.

Another parián called Jaro was formed with a significant weaving industry, agriculture, and brickmaking factories that supported major construction projects and the furniture industry. Due to its wealth and cultural sophistication, Jaro became a religious center, a Catholic diocese with a bishopric, a seminario-colegio, a school for girls (San José), and a fashion center out of its weaving industries managed by its industrious women. Jaro eventually became a ciudad-municipal with a major cathedral and elegant mansions owned by families whose surnames began with the letter "J" or "G" (Javellana, Jardiolin, Jaime, Justiniani, Jalandoni, Javelosa, Genille, Jereos, Jaranilla, Jalbuena, and so on).

From Arévalo, the Spanish conquistadores moved to Iloilo proper (called Catarmán), where they built a ciudad española over the years with a calle real, a church (San José), a school for girls (Sagrado Corazón), a school for boys (San Agustín), a large mercado, a plaza (Alfonso XII), a fortification called Fuerte de San Pedro located at La Cotta (from the Visayan "kuta"), a port or puerto, later called Muelle Loney, a grand Casa Real de Gobierno, a Casino Español, and a Patio Cementerio de Tanza. Most of the Spanish and mestizo families had Spanish Basque surnames beginning with "Y" (Ynza, Yznart, Yber, Ybiernas, Ynchausti, Ysmael, Yberia, Yntalan, Yñon, Yrrezabal, Ygnacio, Yreñeta, Yzasi, Yturriaga, Ybardeloza, Yson, Ynchoa, Ynchon, and so forth). To serve the needs of these original Spanish settlers, many Chinese from Arévalo followed them to the Ciudad Española to open bazaars on Calle Real. Don Pedro Marquez-Lim was the foremost chino cristiano who did this. The native Ylongos, on the other hand, came in by the thousands to become market vendors of dry goods brought in from nearby pueblos.

An old Spanish tower in Villa de Arévalo.

※

ILOILO PROPER QUICKLY evolved into an active trading hub and a cultural center for the performing arts, literature, and entertainment. Its cosmopolitanism was exemplified not only by a significant population of Spanish creoles and mestizos, but also by a large number of British, German, Swiss, and Italian nationals happily socializing with the chinos cristianos of Molo and Jaro, as well as the wealthy indio principalía who frequently visited from nearby coastal municipios such as La Paz, Oton, Pavía, Pototan, Santa Bárbara, and other seaside towns like Dumangas, Ajuy, Lemery, Balasan, and Carles.

As all Ylongo natives and chinos cristianos were Spanish citizens on par with insulares and peninsulares, they mingled freely at numerous patronal fiestas and social gatherings throughout the year, leading to frequent and celebrated intermarriage between the scions of these three communities. This tradition has resulted in the unity that Ylongos enjoy today as a proud legacy.

The harmonious coexistence between races and social classes in Iloilo did not go unnoticed by British Governor-General Sir John Bowring during his visit in the 1870s, which he described in detail in his book, *A Visit to the Philippines*.

John Bowring served as Governor-General of Hong Kong from 1854 to 1859. During his time in the Philippines, he wrote a book detailing his observations and experiences in the country.

> The ties of separation among the classes and the races appeared to me less marked as is the case in other Oriental countries. I saw at the same table Spaniards, Chinese Christians, Indio natives, priests, military men. There is no doubt that having the same religion forms a great bond among so different kinds of people. To the eyes of those who have seen the repulsions and the differences among races in various countries of Asia and for those who know that race is a great divider of people and society, it is admirable to see the absence of racial and caste discriminations among the people of the Philippines.

"Municipio" at Arévalo

The Municipio de Arévalo (circa 1907), the seat of the local government of Villa de Arévalo, the oldest Spanish settlement in Iloilo City. As the town grew, it became a thriving center of commerce and industry, eventually evolving into one of the most livable cities in the country. Today, Iloilo City stands as a testament to the resilience and adaptability of the Ylongos, who have transformed their historic roots into a vibrant and dynamic metropolis.

CHAPTER XVIII
THE ROOT OF RIZAL'S ANTI-FRIAR WRITINGS

In Iloilo City, the founding families' last names begin with the letter "Y" in English or "y griega" in Spanish, or the letter "I" in Greek. Examples of these surnames are Ynchausti, Ynza, Yber, Yñón, Ynson, Yturriaga, Ynco, and Ybiernas. These families descended from Spanish Basques who came to the Philippines or the chinos cristianos, except for Ybiernas, of pure indio Visayan origin. Don Vicente Ybiernas, a comprehensive reader and fluent Spanish speaker, was a celebrated hablista. He was an eloquent orator and occasional writer for *El Heraldo* daily and *El Adalid* newspaper, edited by a Jalandoni from Jaro, another distinguished member of the indio Visayan principalía of old.

Don Vicente was continuously elected as the town gobernadorcillo, presidente, or mayor of Iloilo City. He was a well-built and robust caballero, whose booming voice was often heard at the grand salon of Iloilo's Casino Español. His voice would reverberate with wave after wave of applause and cries of "¡Viva España!" during his vinos de honor speeches commemorating the Día Español de Santiago every twenty-fifth of July.

Don Vicente married Doña Estrella Mapa y Lizares, sister of the famous jurist Plácido Mapa y Lizares. She was one of the granddaughters of landed Doña Enrica Alunan de Lizares from Talisay, Negros Occidental. Both Don Vicente and Doña Estrella were intellectuals who spoke out their minds about current events, history, and culture that generally wielded an influence on the Ylongo mind and judgment. They owned the Iloilo Hotel, facing the city's main square, the historic Plaza Libertad. With his family, they frequently visited the hotel because of Doña Estrella's tasty Molo meriendas. Many Ylongo matrons, including our biological mother Lourdes, adored her spirited tertulias de la semana and her frequently smoky but perfumed madiong and panguingue sessions.

Don Vicente and Doña Estrella's oldest son, Dionisio (Diony), preferred to socialize with some American families in Manila. Diony was friendly and enjoyed more the company of some Clark Air Base American pilots of Chinese and Japanese origin, who resided with their respective families at the Clark Air Base barracks in Pampanga. He headed a "Cultural Exchange Association," where he and his local friends would stay overnight in the camp houses of one or two of his Clark Air Base buddies. While staying as house guests, an interesting exchange, carried out in English over an American-style dinner, would take place. It was a stateside version of the tertulia that touched on modern life and culture that gave exciting insights into the lives of these Asian American servicemen and their families who could stand as models to follow by Filipinos brought up in English.

In the photo, seated are Estrella and Vicente Ybiernas with the three youngest members of their family: Vince, Victor, and Ma. Cristina. Also present is their elder son, Father Bernard, a Catholic priest. Standing behind them are (from the left) Letty and Diony, Marilou and Rene, and Teresita and Manoling.

Diony had a deep fascination with America, which explained his close relationship with Asian Americans. It became evident to those around him that unlike his parents, Diony and his siblings were a new generation of Filipinos who no longer spoke Spanish. Despite understanding the language, their unspoken desire was to eventually settle in America. Diony and his siblings, who included a priest, were becoming Americanized and shedding their Hispanic cultural roots. Don Vicente, Diony's father, was saddened by this development, although he did not openly express it. Don Vicente and his contemporaries were resigned to the changing attitude of their children, though there were times when they clashed. However, they chalked it up to the inevitability of change brought about by the imperial government's "miseducation in English."

Don Vicente represented the native Ylongo Filipino race with its unique character, thoughts, and opinions. He was considered a cultural hero by many elderly Ylongos who remembered him closely. During the Liberation-era years, he went to La Cotta, where the old Spanish-era Fort San Pedro stood, and confronted American bulldozers and army cargo trucks hauling stones from the walls of the fort. He demanded that they stop the demolition, arguing that the fort was a historic landmark that should be respected. Despite the American officers stopping

The San Pedro that exists today bears no resemblance to the La Cotta of the past, as the Spanish-era walls were demolished by American GIs after World War II.

the demolition and taking Don Vicente back to City Hall, they resumed the demolition the following day. Don Vicente later found out that he had been deceived, but he remained silent because he knew that nobody could go against the American "liberators."

On another occasion, Don Vicente questioned the renaming of Iloilo's main street in honor of José María Basa, a merchant who financed the smuggling of Rizal's books into the country. He argued that Basa was not an Ylongo, and the people of the city did not even know him. Don Vicente eventually learned that the Masons in government were responsible for renaming all the main streets in every Filipino town and city after José Rizal. This prompted a different opinion about Rizal to surface.

※

DON VICENTE WAS well aware of the famous old story involving Doña María Felipe de Villanueva, a prominent Ylonga, who vehemently refused to have Rizal stay in her mansion located in the Molo district. Doña María, who was then

In one frame, the three stages of José Rizal's life are depicted—his childhood, youth, and adulthood as an accomplished doctor who gained fame for his critical works against the friars.

known as Molo's queen of the sinamay industry and a papal awardee, refused to accommodate Rizal during his visit to Iloilo because he was a Mason. Rizal had been invited to stay by Doña María's son, Don Emilio Villanueva, who had been Rizal's schoolmate at a Madrid university in the 1880s.

Like Doña María, Don Vicente had also studied the life and works of Rizal. He knew that Rizal had political ambitions to become a Spanish Cortes or parliament member, perhaps to stop their eviction from the hacienda they leased from the Dominicans due to non-payment of rent. Don Vicente concluded that Rizal's political ambition stemmed from a half-brother of his mother, Doña Teodora, who had served in some capacity at the Spanish Cortes in Madrid. Don Vicente also knew that Rizal's father, Don Francisco Mercado, had been a mayor, or gobernadorcillo, of prosperous Biñán, La Laguna, where the wealthy and landed Alberto family dominated the town plaza with their opulent mansion.

Don Vicente correctly psychoanalyzed the young Rizal in Biñán as a resentful child, not only because of his small and short stature but also because of his condition as a poor relative of the rich Albertos of Biñán. When the young José made his family tree, he cut out the Alberto branch out of hatred. Moreover, there is no record indicating that the boy Rizal was ever received well in the Alberto mansion while studying under a town maestro named Salustiano Aquino. The boy Rizal was never known to have stayed in the Alberto mansion where his mother was once accused of trying to poison her sister-in-law. The latter called the police, who promptly arrested her and made her walk to the Santa Cruz town courthouse and jail. She was pronounced guilty and sat in prison for two years.

The perceptive boy Rizal realized that the Albertos were proud of their social status as genuine landowners, while he was the son of mere lessees of a friar hacienda, from which they could be thrown out anytime by the actual owners. This reality rankled in Rizal's mind since his childhood in Biñán and when he wrote his anti-friar hate articles and novels. Don Vicente analyzed Rizal's true motives for attacking the Spanish friars, stating that the motive was never "love of country" but plain self-interest, sectarian, and racist hatred, or plain Hispanophobia, which was evident in his novels, *La Solidaridad* essays, and articles.

The reality of Rizal's resentment was apparent when the ejectment case decision was implemented, and Rizal and his family were no longer staying in their Calamba mansion. They had already abandoned it, with his parents residing anew in Binondo, Manila, his mother in a house on Calle San Fernando, and his father in another house on Calle Estraude. Twenty-five other families were removed from the Calamba hacienda premises, who claimed to be individuals under the employ of the Rizal family and possibly also Masons and Katipunan members.

The luxurious Hotel Oriente.

However, the details about this ejectment case were deliberately omitted in every Rizal biography.

According to the Americanized education, Rizal returned to Manila in 1892 with his widowed sister Lucia from Hong Kong, determined to lead a reform movement through the Liga Filipina he hoped to establish. He stayed in the luxurious Binondo Hotel Oriente for pre-arranged personal audiences with then Governor-General Eulogio Despujol, who even sent his official Palace carruaje to pick him up from the hotel and to drive him back. Don Vicente claimed that during these audiences, the Governor-General, a Mason like Rizal, tried to convince him that he and his family could have any other hacienda anywhere in the Philippines except their lost Calamba lands. Don Vicente believed that Rizal was "playing hard to get" by insisting on claiming the Calamba hacienda, but the Governor-General could not defy the court that had already ruled in favor of the Dominicans. The revelation that there was an attempt to placate him and his family tells us that there was an effort to resolve the issue. However, while discussing these topics, a report emerged about Rizal's anti-Pope Masonic leaflets, which were allegedly found hidden inside pillowcases in Lucia's luggage by Customs.

After the controversial leaflet incident, the Governor-General saw an opportunity to exile Rizal to Dapitan for four years. It was believed that Rizal and his family would settle down there, but his parents and siblings decided to remain in the city. Even though he was separated from his loved ones, Rizal expressed in his writings that he was content and happy in Dapitan.

Despite being in exile in Dapitan, Rizal remained aware of the political situation in the Philippines. The Katipunan had already been formed in Manila in 1892, and its members were planning a revolution against Spanish rule.

In June 1896, the Katipunan sent Pio Valenzuela to Dapitan to try and persuade Rizal to support their cause. Bonifacio saw Rizal as a symbol of the Filipino nation and believed that his support would lend legitimacy to their revolution.

However, Rizal, who had always advocated for peaceful reform rather than violent revolution, was wary of the Katipunan's methods. He also feared for his own safety, as he knew that being associated with the Katipunan could lead to his arrest or even execution.

Instead, Rizal decided to offer his services as a volunteer doctor for the Spanish army in Cuba. He believed that by doing so, he could demonstrate his loyalty to Spain and perhaps gain the support of Spanish authorities for his own reformist agenda.

Governor-General Eulogio Despujol: A figure of controversy in Philippine history, remembered for exiling José Rizal to Dapitan.

Rizal's offer to serve as a volunteer doctor in the Spanish army in Cuba was granted, and he eagerly requested to leave his Dapitan exile and travel to Manila. From there, he embarked on a journey to Barcelona to fulfill his commitment to the Spanish authorities. However, upon arrival, he was arrested by the authorities and accused of leading the revolutionary movement in the Philippines.

After his arrest in Barcelona, Rizal was promptly sent back to Manila, where he faced a series of charges, including sedition, rebellion, and conspiracy.

The Katipunan falsely accused him of being their leader and inspiration. This resulted in his recall from Barcelona and charges of illicit association and rebellion. During his trial, Rizal vehemently denied favoring the Katipunan uprising, but unfortunately, his explanation that the rebels were not yet ready to revolt proved fatal to his case. The court concluded that he was not against the uprising, leading to his tragic execution by firing squad.

In the years that followed, the American government implemented a revisionist history that portrayed Rizal as a hero and used him for their local propaganda purposes. Despite this, Rizal's legacy lives on as a symbol of resistance against oppression and a testament to the power of words and ideas.

CHAPTER XIX
REVISING HISTORY TO SERVE NEOCOLONIALISM

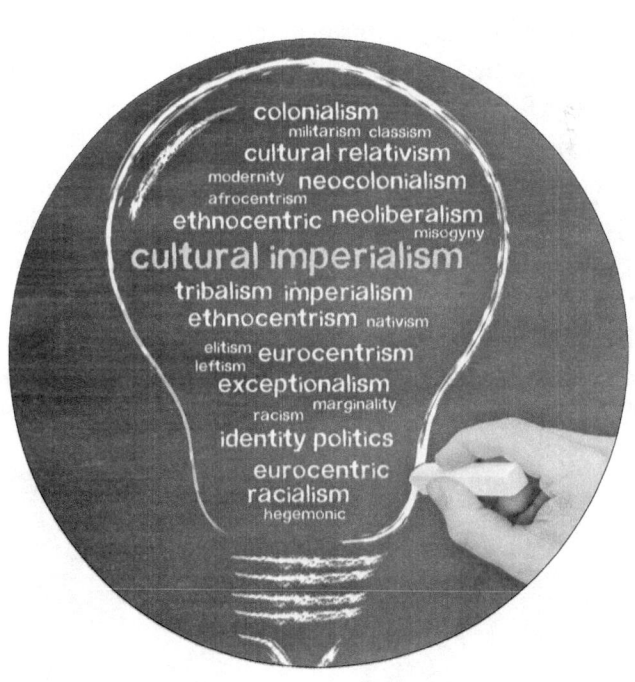

On May 2022, Ferdinand Marcos y Romuáldez was elected as the new President of the Philippines, thirty-six years after his father's ouster from power. His unprecedented landslide victory garnered over thirty million votes, representing more than fifty-eight percent of the total votes cast.

However, Marcos' ascension to the highest office was met with concerns from his opponents who fear that he would revise history to conceal the abuses of his father's fourteen-year reign of martial law. The Marcos regime's legacy has always been a subject of debate, with supporters and critics having differing opinions. While some argue that the population may have collectively benefited from Ferdinand Marcos y Edralín Sr.'s rule, others condemn the rampant corruption and human rights violations committed during his tenure.

Moreover, the issue of the Marcos family's alleged ill-gotten wealth remains a significant question that must be objectively addressed to ensure justice. The lingering allegations against the Marcoses suggest that they may have illegally acquired their wealth at the expense of the public coffers.

Despite the controversies surrounding the Marcoses, they have been given a second chance, and their victory has been seen as a repudiation of the Aquino-Cojuangco political dynasty and the People Power Revolution of 1986, which cat-

In May 2022, Ferdinand Romuáldez Marcos Jr. won an unparalleled and overwhelming victory, becoming the seventeenth president of the Republic of the Philippines.

apulted Corazon C. Aquino to power. The Aquino-Marcos feud has long divided the nation, leaving it vulnerable to external political manipulation.

The Filipino people have become a nation divided, serving the interests of puppet masters, with American neocolonialists pulling the strings behind the scenes through their local assets. The United States has been exercising immense power over the destiny of developing nations, such as the Philippines, through lending institutions, enabling it to maintain its status as a world superpower.

The external debt situation of the Philippines has only worsened with the Covid-19 pandemic, and the country now owes, as of this writing, a staggering amount of ₱12.89 trillion to the International Monetary Fund and other creditors. The Marcos presidency now faces the enormous task of addressing the country's economic challenges and navigating its relationship with external forces.

⚜

PRESIDENT MARCOS WOULD be wise to heed the lessons of history and avoid becoming entangled in the United States' latest geopolitical gamesmanship. The U.S. government has been ramping up tensions with China in the Asia-Pacific region, and Marcos must be careful not to let himself be used as a pawn in this new Cold War.

It is worth noting that the U.S. has a checkered history in the Philippines, and that the ouster of Marcos' father in 1986 was just one example of their meddling in the country's affairs. The U.S. has a long history of interfering in the Philippines, after the country gained its independence in 1946.

In contrast, Spain, as a colonial power, took a different approach to the Philippines. While the American tack was to impose its own culture and values on the Philippines, Spain's attitude was to introduce European civilization and culture to the local people. This was done through the efforts of Spanish Catholic missionaries, who accompanied every expedition and evangelized the newly-conquered territories.

This approach gave rise to new nations, such as the Philippines, which were introduced to European culture and civilization. The Spanish conquest of the Philippines came with the Sword and the Cross, and while there were certainly negative aspects to this approach, it also had its benefits.

Spain's colonial policy can be viewed as benevolent, given the lasting impact it had on the Philippines. Presently, the Philippines stands as a leading predominantly Catholic nation in Asia, which is a testament to Spain's endeavors to Christianize the native populace.

So while Marcos must be cautious about getting involved in the new Cold War, he should also remember the positive aspects of the country's Spanish colonial past. By recognizing the lasting influence of Spain on the Philippines, Marcos can chart a course that is both independent and respectful of the country's cultural heritage.

For over three hundred years, the Philippines had enjoyed the benefits of European civilization until the U.S. mother lodge of Masons orchestrated an anti-friar Katipunan revolution in the 1890s. This was done as a prelude to the actual invasion and occupation of the Philippines by the American forces. The nefarious Masonic scheme included the drafting of José Rizal as a propagandist and Emilio Aguinaldo as the leader of its military arm. *Behind the Lodge Door*, a meticulously-researched book by Paul A. Fisher, a former high-ranking American Mason, exposed the conspiracy to the world. According to Fisher's documented evidence, the Masons not only sought to de-Christianize America but also other nations such as Italy, Germany, France, Japan, China, and the Philippines.

As Father Vincent Miceli, a former professor at the Gregorian and Angelicum universities in Rome, pointed out, Fisher's book was "a brilliant exposé of the hidden power that Freemasonry has in the past and still is exerting so successfully to de-Christianize America." However, some historians, both Filipino and American, including Jesuits, ignore this basic fact when they idealize the Katipunan and characterize the entire Filipino clergy of the 1890s as "revolutionary." This idealization is far from the truth, for neither the Katipunan nor the entire Filipino clergy was revolutionary. The Katipunan was a spy organization created by the war-mongering American Masons, and only a sprinkling of Filipino clergy was involved. The Visayan clergy of that era generally never sympathized with the Katipunan.

Although some clergymen supported the Masons for pushing revolutionary ideas against Spain, they were not revolutionary themselves. Padre José Apolonio Burgos, a Spanish Creole who was executed for his alleged involvement in the Cavite Mutiny in 1872, was one such clergyman. As *masonrytoday.com* notes, Padre Burgos was not a Mason himself, "although he was, for lack of a better term, on the side of the Freemasons in the Philippines at the time mostly because [of their] involvement in the Revolution and their opposition to the despotic rule of the Spanish Friars who Burgos also opposed. He was close friends with Paciano Rizal, José Rizal's older brother. José Rizal was a Freemason and very active in the Revolution activities of the time. A Chapter of Rose Croix of the Ancient Accepted Scottish in the Philippines is named for Burgos."

Gregorio Aglipay, founder of the Philippine Independent Church, was made a Mason in Lodge Magdalo in Aguinaldo's native Cavite in 1918. However, both Burgos and Aglipay were the exceptions. In general, the Filipino clergy of the 1890s did not support the Katipunan, and the idea that they were revolutionary is simply a myth perpetuated by those who wish to rewrite history to suit their

THE INDEPENDENT HISTORY OF YLONGO AND CEBUANO VISAYANS

The Masonic square and compasses symbol can be found encrusted in the main floor of the Scottish Rite of Freemasonry headquarters in Washington, D.C.

own agenda. The majority of the Filipino clergy remained loyal to their faith and country, and did not participate in the anti-friar Katipunan revolution.

It is important to note that the Spanish approach to colonization, though certainly not perfect, had a different aim than the American strategy. The Spanish sought to spread Christianity and European civilization to the lands they conquered, while the Americans pursued economic and political domination.

The American invasion and occupation of the Philippines resulted in the deaths of over a million Filipinos, the destruction of entire cities, and the subjugation of the Filipino people to American rule. This was all done in the name of "benevolent assimilation," a concept which, in reality, was anything but benevolent.

The involvement of Freemasonry in the anti-friar Katipunan revolution is a little-known fact that has been glossed over in many historical accounts. This is due in part to the fact that many of the "historians" who have written about this period in Philippine history have been influenced by the same Masonic agenda that sought to de-Christianize the Philippines and other nations.

In the end, it is important for us to know the truth about our history, even if that truth is uncomfortable or inconvenient. We must not allow ourselves to be manipulated by those who seek to rewrite history for their own purposes. Instead, we must seek the truth, no matter where it leads us, and use that truth to build a better future for ourselves and our country.

CHAPTER XX
CAN WE TRUST AMERICA'S 'STRATEGIC AMBIGUITY'?

President Joseph Biden of the United States has vowed military intervention in the event of a Chinese attack on Taiwan, which China considers a renegade province. However, the frequent air and sea incursions by China across the Taiwan Strait have left the Taiwanese people feeling nervous and apprehensive. Although the United States maintains a One China policy recognizing the People's Republic of China as the only legal government of China and Taiwan as part of China, it does not concede Chinese sovereignty over Taiwan.

Despite Biden's commitment to defending Taiwan militarily, U.S. officials have clarified that nothing has changed regarding America's long-standing "strategic ambiguity" policy toward Taiwan. This policy allows the United States to maintain formal relations with China while having unofficial relations with Taiwan, keeping its options open.

The apprehension of ordinary Taiwanese has increased following Russia's invasion of Ukraine, which led to millions of Ukrainian refugees fleeing to other countries. Ukraine had apparently believed the U.S. and the North Atlantic Treaty Organization (NATO) would send troops to defend Ukraine in case of a Russian invasion, and that Ukraine would be accepted as a NATO member and made a part of the European Union. However, when the time came, the United States and NATO did not send troops but instead provided Ukraine with Soviet-era weapons from former Warsaw Pact nations now part of NATO.

Many ordinary Taiwanese are beginning to see themselves in a similar position to the fleeing Ukrainians. Given the experience of Emilio Aguinaldo with American duplicity (strategic ambiguity), the Taiwanese have reason to doubt America's resolve. They believe that the U.S. is using Taiwan to undermine China and maintain dominance in the Asia-Pacific region, similar to how they utilized Aguinaldo to defeat Spain during the Spanish-American War of 1898, which marked the end of the Spanish empire.

※

ALTHOUGH OUR HISTORY textbooks never prominently mention the Voluntarios for Spain, the American invaders never dismissed the possibility of Aguinaldo joining Spain's forces as a Voluntario to repel and kick out Admiral George Dewey's forces from Manila. This fear prompted the Americans to seek out Aguinaldo in Hong Kong to win him over to their side, using their Masonic connections as we have already pointed out in previous chapters. Aguinaldo's emissary to win support for Philippine independence, Felipe Agoncillo, and his intermediary with the Spanish authorities for a truce formalized by the Pact of Biacnabató, Pedro Paterno, advised Aguinaldo to side with Spain. Had they succeeded in getting Aguinaldo to help Spain against the fewer American forces, the invading Americans would have been unable to take away the Philippines. However, Aguinaldo naively believed in the American promise (a Masonic pact) of independence and trusted their word that once Spain was ejected from the archipelago with his help, they would allow him to lead the independent Philippines. He quickly declared Philippine independence from Spain on June 12, 1898.

However, the Americans never fulfilled their promise, foreshadowing their current policy of "strategic ambiguity." Aguinaldo did his part of the bargain, cornering the Spanish forces on land while Dewey's forces blockaded Manila Bay. Filipino forces captured 5,000 Spanish troops and laid siege to Intramuros to starve the last Spanish holdouts. The Americans, buoyed by fresh reinforcements, no longer had any use for Aguinaldo. They negotiated with the Spaniards for their peaceful surrender to the Americans, keeping Aguinaldo in the dark about their blatant betrayal. An American general involved in the conflict articulated their low regard for Filipinos. According to Theodore S. Gonzalves' *The Day the Dancers Stayed: Performing in the Filipino/American Diaspora* (Temple University Press, 2009), as adapted in a short article that appeared in *americanhistory.si.edu*, this is how it went down:

General Wesley Merritt

> During negotiations between Dewey's camp and [the Spanish commander], U.S. Army General Wesley Merritt, commander of the San Francisco–based VIII Corps, shared his views of Filipinos. In an 1899 interview, Merritt told a journalist from the *New York Sun* that he had come 'with orders not to treat with the Indians [sic]; not to recognize them, and not to promise anything,' adding, General 'Aguinaldo is just the same to me as a boy [a derogatory term for a black man] in the street.'

According to some estimates, as many as three million Filipinos died as a result of the Philippine-American War, which was attributed to America's betrayal. However, official U.S. estimates suggest a much lower death toll of as few as two hundred thousand. This war also resulted in the terrible plunder of the Philippine national treasury, with up to one hundred billion U.S. dollars in gold and silver reserves taken. These reserves were accumulated from two hundred and

After a mock battle between Spanish and American forces to deceive General Emilio Aguinaldo and his army, U.S. troops raise the American flag over Fort Antonio Abad in Malate, Manila, following the Spanish surrender of the city to the Americans instead of their former colonial charges.

fifty years of the Galleon Trade, which was a Spanish-Chinese partnership now known as the "First Globalization." Present-day Binondo Chinese Filipinos should be reminded of the generally positive aspects of their Spanish past and Hispanic chino-cristiano culture, although the ugly underbelly of the same past should also be acknowledged, such as the inexcusable 1603 massacre of thousands of Chinese due to immigration and trade rivalry issues.

Aguinaldo would have been better off siding with Spain and its Visayan Leales Voluntarios instead of believing in the American policy of "strategic ambiguity." If he had done so, Spain would have given him true Philippine independence, as they did in the case of Equatorial Guinea. Many other former Spanish possessions could have also achieved independence without so much bloodshed and other iniquities that followed the advent of American imperialism.

Despite the lessons of 1898, Filipinos never learned. The Americanized Filipinos of the 1930s relied on the old version of the same American policy of "strategic ambiguity" during the 1941 Japanese invasion. As a reward for their faith in the American promise of protection, the country experienced near-total devastation at the end of the Second World War. This included the destruction of the priceless Walled City of Intramuros by American forces, which has taken close to eighty years to rehabilitate with no end in sight.

There is a possibility of communist China invading Taiwan to reclaim its sovereignty over what it considers a renegade province. If war breaks out, the Philippines could get involved given the communist giant's continued aggressive

Felipe Agoncillo

The photo above shows American soldiers making their way toward Manila along the seashore during the mock battle aimed at capturing the city. In the photo below, a Filipino revolutionary can be seen holding on to a cannon captured from the Spanish, while entrenched in bamboo.

Pedro Paterno

moves in the West Philippine Sea. Despite the "ironclad" commitment of the U.S. to defend the Philippines in the event of an attack on any Philippine vessels or claimed territories in the disputed West Philippine Sea, Filipinos are uncertain if the U.S. would follow through on its pledge. The U.S. response to an attack on the Philippines is subject to approval by the U.S. Congress. The verbiage in the 1951 Mutual Defense Treaty between the U.S. and its former colonial charge is unclear on how quickly the U.S. could respond. Thus, Filipinos should be cautious when they hear the phrase "strategic ambiguity."

CHAPTER XXI
VISAYAN SENSE OF UNITY REMAINS UNSHAKABLE

To achieve progress as a nation, it is necessary for us to unite and put our political differences aside for the sake of our country and people. The Americans adopted a "divide and rule" policy in the 1900s, after crushing any resistance to their rule, which should not have a place in our society as it creates division among Filipinos.

The Philippine-American War lasted three years, starting in 1899 and ending in 1902 when General Miguel Malvar surrendered. However, for the victorious Americans, the war never truly ended. Instead, they implemented a more insidious approach through the educational system to brainwash generations of Filipinos for over a hundred years.

The American colonialists waged a cultural and linguistic war against the Filipino people by enforcing English as the medium of education, which has fractured the national unity forged by over three hundred years of Catholic and Spanish influence. This second phase of the Philippine-American War aimed to confuse and stupefy the new and rising generations of Filipinos, resulting in the country's indebtedness to trillions of pesos in foreign loan obligations, violent patronal and dynastic politics, and institutionalized bureaucratic corruption at all levels of society and government.

The goal of this mess is to exploit economically the Filipinos who are getting poorer and poorer, while their politicians can be manipulated with bribery or controlled by the U.S. government.

Today, the majority of Filipinos suffer from intellectual and financial poverty, as evidenced by the Tagalog Abakada puristas in government who believe that the country's name is "Pilipinas" instead of "Filipinas" because Filipinos supposedly do not have the letter F in their alphabet or cannot pronounce the F sound.

To defend the preservation of the Spanish language for the cultural and economic good of future Filipinos, all the authors of legislative bills are Visayans. Congressman Pascual B. Azanza from Samar-Leyte filed the first bill for teaching Spanish in the primary grades. Senator Vicente Sotto y Yap from Cebu authored a bill including Spanish as a high school subject, but it was undermined by the American-controlled Department of Education.

Senator Enrique Magalona from Iloilo and Negros authored a law requiring college students to take twelve units of Spanish, and Miguel Cuenco from the Parián of Cebu authored the law requiring college students to earn twenty-four units of Spanish studies, which were later abolished by the Tagalog Abakada puristas.

The "divide and rule policy" of the American colonialists targeted the culture and language of the Filipinos of the 1898 Aguinaldo República. Interestingly, Spanish is widely spoken and taught in all American schools, and even Netflix movies today are all dubbed in Spanish, but it is taboo for Filipinos to learn Spanish.

The Tagalog Abakada puristas continue to oppose Spanish, which unites Tagalogs with Visayans, Pampangos, Ilocanos, Bicolanos, Mindananaons, and others who are for national unity. However, with their inanity, it won't be long for a wise future government to abolish the Komisyon sa Wikang Filipino because it is deemed irrelevant and useless.

All in all, it is important for Filipinos to recognize the impact of language and culture on their national identity and unity. The American colonialists' "divide and rule" policy, which aimed to confuse and exploit Filipinos, has left a lasting legacy on the country's economic and political systems.

However, it is not too late to reclaim the Filipino identity and reunite as a nation. The preservation and promotion of Spanish, as well as other Filipino languages, can serve as a unifying force that transcends regional and cultural differences.

It is time for Filipinos to come together and work toward a common goal of progress and prosperity for the country and its people. Let us set aside our political differences and focus on the bigger picture—the future of the Philippines.

CHAPTER XXII
HOW LARGE-SCALE CORRUPTION STARTED

The reason we use the term "Pilipino corruption" instead of "Filipino corruption" is that the most corrupt officials in the government are the Abakada puristas, or 'Pilipinos', who are influenced by the invented Lope K. Santos Abakada purist culture. This culture is one of the main strategies used by American colonial-era official Dean C. Worcester in his crusade to stupefy and corrupt the Filipinos. Worcester was the complainant in the libel case arising from the 1908 "Aves de rapiña" editorial. He was the one who ordered Santos to invent the Abakada to push back the already civilized Spanish-speaking Filipinos to their pre-Hispanic culture. Many Filipinos were already Ilustrados (Enlightened Ones) at that time and were educated in some of the best European universities, particularly in Spain. The idea of turning back the hands of time and bringing modern Filipinos back to their pre-Hispanic primitive and savage civilization is disturbing.

Before Worcester was appointed to his juicy posts in the Philippines, he had already seeded the minds of U.S. policymakers and powerful politicians with the racist idea that Filipinos were incapable of self-governance and did not deserve independence. Worcester was born in 1866 in Vermont and died in 1924. He had an early fascination with nature and pursued his interest in birds by enrolling in zoology at the University of Michigan, where he graduated in 1889. He met zoology Professor Joseph Steere during his sophomore year who was planning an expedition to the Philippines to study bird species in the islands. Worcester became Steere's assistant in the 1889 expedition and gained practical knowledge about the archipelago. Years later, this experience would prove useful when another professor introduced him to President William McKinley, which led to his appointment as a member of the Philippine Commission, the executive and legislative body tasked to govern the Philippines during the early years of American colonial rule.

Worcester served as the interior secretary at one time for the Insular Government of the Philippine Islands. As the interior secretary, he allegedly allowed the processing of diseased meat for human consumption, conducted controversial studies of the Igorots, and used these studies as a smokescreen for gold prospecting. He also sold lands in Mindoro, which led to the exploitation of the Mangyan tribe in the area. Barbara A. West, in her book *Encyclopedia of the Peoples of Asia and Oceania* (Infobase Publishing, 2010), linked Worcester to the misery that plagued the Mangyans of Mindoro for decades after he arranged for the sale of vast tracts of land to an American sugar company that employed Mangyans as laborers and exploited them for years. During the American occupation, the authorities moved

A 1908 editorial cartoon portrays two overweight Americans dragging a frail Juan de la Cruz and compelling him to cough up pesos from his mouth.

the Mangyans to reservations similar to those created for Native American Indians in the United States.

In 1899, Worcester ingratiated himself before a group of Republicans during a speech in Illinois that portrayed the Filipinos badly. He also attempted to revise history by mischaracterizing Emilio Aguinaldo's agreement with the Americans in Hong Kong to help them against Spain in exchange for independence. The University of Michigan has a website regarding the university and its relationship with the world, including the Philippines. It includes an article that tells us more about Worcester's character, especially his inability to tell the truth.

> At the turn of the 20th century, the United States acquired the territories of Cuba, Guam, Puerto Rico, and the Philippines from Spain, as stipulated in the Treaty of Paris following the Spanish-American War. Among the US government, scholars, elites, and the public, a question arose: what should the United States do with the newly-acquired Philippines?
>
> One influential contributor to the debate was Dean Conant Worcester, notable not only for his strong ties to the University of Michigan but also for his extensive trips and first-hand experience in the Philippines. Worcester attended the U-M from 1884 to 1889, during which he was a part of Joseph Beal Steere's expedition to the Philippines. He graduated with a degree in zoology and later worked as an Assistant Professor at UM. Because of his involvement with the Philippine expedition, Worcester was considered to be among the most knowledgeable about the country, and his works and speeches helped shape the perception of the territory for the general American public. Thanks to his status as a Michigan alumnus and donations from his fam-

ily, the Bentley Historical Library holds an extensive collection related to Worcester, his notes, and his published work.

Dean Worcester used his prominence and status to promote a pro-imperialist message. On November 15, 1899, he gave a speech to the Hamilton Club at Central Music Hall in Chicago. Though only recently established, the Hamilton Club was already well-known as a Republican party social club and meeting place. Members congregated to discuss political topics in addition to enjoying the amenities that the club had to offer. As a political meeting ground, the Hamilton Club became influential in elections and political issues, especially when the Republican National Convention was held in Chicago. When Worcester gave his speech in November of 1899, the national presidential elections were less than a year away. He knew that the subject of imperialism in the Philippines and his thoughts on the matter would appeal to the crowd of Republicans.

Worcester's speech to the Hamilton Club focused on discrediting the legitimacy of the Republic of the Philippines (declared after the Philippines war against Spain, in 1899), emphasizing the positive influence of American leaders, and diminishing the fact of hostility between Filipinos and Americans. His speech took place in the context of an ongoing, brutal war between the US and the Philippine revolutionaries throughout the archipelago.

First, Worcester claimed that Emilio Aguinaldo, the first president of the Republic of the Philippines, was not promised independence from Admiral Dewey, the leader of the American forces in the Philippines. Worcester cited letters that Aguinaldo wrote to US President William McKinley that failed to mention any American promise of Philippine independence. According to Worcester, Aguinaldo insisted that no American promised to grant the Philippines its independence. Worcester attempted to set the record straight against characterizations of American dishonesty.

Another of Worcester's arguments, especially in response to anti-imperialist criticism, was that the Philippines was worse off under Spanish rule and would have continued on a similar path if Aguinaldo and other Tagalog leaders were in power. Worcester pointed out that after the Philippine Revolution in 1897, Aguinaldo accepted a large sum of money and amnesty from the Spanish government and in exchange the revolutionary government was exiled to Hong Kong. Aguinaldo then put this sum of money in his personal bank account. Worcester contrasted Aguinaldo's selfish and dishonest actions against those of a 'legitimate' government: the United States. In painting Aguinaldo as corrupt, Worcester sought to demonstrate that Filipino leaders only had their own interests in mind and therefore lacked the capacity to govern their own people.

At the same time, Worcester attempted to prove that the Filipinos were allies of the Americans before the capture of Manila. He argued, for example, that the American Army did infinitely more than Aguinaldo's army in driving out and destroying Spanish power, and that the Americans were just trying to help the Filipinos achieve sovereignty. Worcester's claim of alliance was tenuous at best, as there was never any true cooperation between American and Filipino forces. Worcester then contradicted himself, later mentioning that the situation in the Philippines grew worse as so-called Filipino "insurgents" became more hostile toward Americans after the fall of Manila. An instance of this hostility came when an American sentry killed a Filipino, prompting retaliation, which resulted in more Filipinos who died.

Dean Conant Worcester

The Americans never intended to declare war, according to Worcester. The Philippine-American War was just the unfortunate result of misunderstanding America's good intention to support Filipinos in their eventual self-governance. His message repeatedly laid blame for the conflict between Filipinos and Americans at the Filipinos' feet. To a Republican audience, this speech may have been well-received. Worcester packaged US imperialism in ways that erased American violence, exploitation, and arrogance while aggrandizing America's civilizing mission and sense of self-importance. For Americans who believed Worcester's claims, US imperialism in the Philippines was an extension of American humanitarianism and good will. (Source: *https://philippines.michiganintheworld.history.lsa.umich.edu/s/exhibit/page/dean-worcester-pro-imperialist-message*.)

WORCESTER PLAYED A pivotal role in demonizing the Spaniards to pave the way for American imperialism in the Philippines. His aim was to convince Filipinos that the Spaniards were the enemy in order to strengthen America's shaky control over the population. His actions were driven by Hispanophobia. He enforced the policy of historical revisionism among the new generation of Filipinos, portraying Magellan as an "invader," when in fact, he arrived in Cebu accidentally.

Worcester also initiated the practice of native language engineering, using Lope K. Santos to teach schoolchildren the invented purista Abakada to remove Spanish words that had already been integrated into native languages, such as Tagalog. This policy aimed to promote intellectual poverty among native children.

An archived copy of "Aves de rapiña," which was printed on October 30, 1908, is available at Filipinas Heritage Library.

Due to this deliberate miseducation, the new generations are not aware of the historical truth behind the pidgin Taglish they speak today. The students are misled and taught to focus only on a fictional character called Padre Dámaso, created by Rizal, as their national enemy, while the real enemies like Worcester are kept hidden from them. Fortunately, the Visayans, especially the Ylongos and Cebuanos, were mostly immune to this detrimental influence because their local government officials were not generally corrupt. They had inherited solid Spanish values such as delicadeza, amor propio, and palabra de honor, which made it impossible for them to engage in shenanigans and venalities.

At the time of this writing, the Philippine media was busy exposing the disappearance of the multibillion-peso budget allocated for vaccines and equipment to combat the Covid-19 Delta variant. Some government officials educated in English were shamelessly involved in this blatant corruption. This kind of large-scale criminality was unheard of during the Spanish dominion because what Filipinos understand today as corruption started under the American regime.

When the editorial "Aves de rapiña" was published on October 30, 1908, Worcester was at the height of his influence as a high official of the American colonial government. It was written in Spanish by Fidel A. Reyes, city editor of the nationalist daily *El Renacimiento Filipino* and published by Teodoro M. Kálaw, the paper's chief editor. Reyes wrote it after hearing about Worcester's alleged rapacity. Worcester knew he was guilty of the corruption exposed and denounced by the mentioned Filipino journalists in Spanish.

Tagalogs and Visayans were united as one people by the Spanish language. Their political and cultural opposition was linked against the undemocratic imposition of English as the compulsory official language and the only medium of instruction in all schools. They were initially a Spanish-speaking nation trying to recover from the horrors of the bloody American war against the Aguinaldo República de Filipinas.

Discerning Tagalogs and Visayans knew what Worcester was trying to do. United by the Spanish language and their Hispanic patrimony, they opposed his moves. He paid opportunistic Tagalogs like Lope K. Santos to reinvent and purify the native languages, which was an attack on their culture and native languages. The Abakada purista mania that Worcester unleashed corrupted government ser-

BIRDS OF PREY

On the surface of this globe, some people are born to eat and devour, others to be eaten and devoured.

Now and then, the latter bestir themselves, endeavoring to rebel against an order of things which makes them prey to, and food of, the insatiable voracity of the former. Sometimes they are fortunate in successfully putting to flight the eaters and devourers; but in the majority cases, the latter only gain a new name or plumage.

The situation is the same everywhere; the relationship existing between the one and the other is that dictated by a too keen appetite, the satisfaction of which must always be at another fellow-creature's expense.

Among men, it is easy to observe the development of this daily phenomenon. And for some psychological reason, nations who believe themselves powerful take the fiercest and most harmful of creatures as their symbol. Such as the lion, or the eagle, or the serpent. Some have done this on a secret impulse of affinity; others, because it has served them as some sort of stimulant to an inflated vanity, the wish to make themselves appear that which they are not nor will ever be.

The eagle, symbolizing liberty and strength, has found the most admirers. And men, collectively and individually, have ever desired to copy and imitate this most rapacious of birds in order to succeed in the plundering of their fellowmen.

But there is a man who, besides being like the eagle, also has the characteristics of the vulture, the owl and the vampire.

He ascends the mountains of Benguet ostensibly to classify and measure Igorot skulls, to study and civilize the Igorots; but, at the same time, he also espies during his flight, with the keen eye of the bird of prey, where the large deposits of gold are, the real prey concealed in the lonely mountains, and then he appropriates these all to himself afterwards, thanks to the legal facilities he can make and unmake at will, always, however, redounding to his own benefit.

He authorizes, despite laws and ordinances to the contrary, the illegal slaughter of diseased cattle so as to make a profit from its infected and putrid meat, which he himself should have condemned in his official capacity.

He presents himself on all occasions with the wrinkled brow of a scientist, who has spent his life deep in the mysteries of the laboratory of science; when in truth, his only scientific work has been the dissection of insects and the importation of fish eggs, as though fish in this country are of so little nourishment and savoriness that they deserve replacement by species from other climes.

He gives laudable impetus to the search of rich lodes in Mindanao, in Mindoro, and in other virgin regions of the archipelago, a search undertaken with the people's money, and with the excuse of its being for the public good; when, in strict truth, his purpose is to obtain data and discover the keys to the national wealth for his essentially personal benefit, as proved by the acquisition of immense properties registered under the names of others.

He promotes through secret agents and partners, the sale to the city of worthless lands at fabulous prices, which the city fathers dare not refuse for fear of displeasing him.

He sponsors concessions for hotels on filled-in lands, with the prospect of enormous profits at the expense of the people.

Such are the characteristics of this man who is also an eagle, who surprises first and then later devours, a vulture who gorges himself on the dead and putrid meats, an owl who affects a petulant omniscience, and a vampire who silently sucks his victims bloodless.

Birds of prey always triumph. Their flight and aim are never thwarted. For who can dare stop them?

There are some who share in the booty and the plunder itself, but the rest are merely too weak to raise a voice of protest. Some die in the disheartening destruction of their own energies and interests. Yet, at the end, there shall appear, with terrifying clearness, that immortal warning of old: Mene, Mene, Tekel, Upharsin.

After publishing "Aves de rapiña," Fidel Alejandro Reyes' paper was compelled to close down due to censorship imposed by the American government.

vice itself. It destroyed Tagalog in the long run, turning it into a pidgin called Taglish. It is a complicated language to master because of its coined Balarila or grammar semantics that are difficult to learn for most Filipinos, regardless of whether or not they are native Tagalog speakers.

Over time, non-Tagalog Filipinos began to distance themselves from the puristas, particularly those who were Visayan. This group fell out of favor with influential delegates of the 1971-73 Constitutional Convention, which was tasked with drafting a new charter for the country. Unfortunately, their fall from grace was a harsh one. Most of the members of the National Language Committee abolished Abakada and Pilipino Balarila and the then Surian ng Wikang Pambansa. Instead, they replaced the language agency with the Komisyon sa Wikang Filipino.

It became apparent that non-Tagalogs would always tend to reveal their original national identity as Filipinos. This was due to the fraud of reinventing Tagalog by replacing its integrated Spanish influence, like silla, with ridiculous Abakada-Balarila word coinages like salumpuwit and hag-himu-in. The Tagalog Abakada puristas turned out to be a language monster from which all non-Tagalogs had to defend their original native ethnicity. This was particularly true for Cebuano and Ylongo Visayans born of the fusion of their Hispanic and indigenous past.

In essence, the Tagalog puristas had unnecessarily de-Hispanized themselves with their culture. They had betrayed the already generalized Hispanic heritage of Filipinos. The Tagalog puristas had no right to mislead and colonize non-Tagalogs. They had no right to force people to embrace their eccentricities, like their mindless and false claim that Filipinos were incapable of articulating or writing the letter F.

Non-Tagalog Filipinos felt that they were being forced to embrace a language and culture that did not represent them. Instead, they wanted to celebrate their unique heritage and their fusion of indigenous and Hispanic culture. The Tagalog puristas had failed to recognize this, and in doing so, they had alienated themselves from the rest of the Filipino population.

Ultimately, the rejection of the Tagalog puristas by non-Tagalog Filipinos was not only a rejection of a particular language but also a rejection of a cultural ideology that sought to impose a narrow definition of Filipino identity. Non-Tagalog Filipinos recognized that their identity was more complex and more diverse than what the puristas were willing to accept. In the end, it was this rejection that paved the way for a more inclusive and diverse understanding of what it means to be Filipino.

CHAPTER XXIII
CLASSIC YLONGO POETRY IS TRUE TO SPANISH FORM

Tradition has made the Ylongo language synonymous with "malambing." The Spanish missionaries of yore referred to it as "dulce, mimosa y acariciante" (coy, sweet, and caressing). In its mellifluous accents, Ylongo reveals not only the inherent warmth and sensuality of a race begotten by the brown earth but a poetic and cultural ancestry hardly equaled by its sister tongues.

If logic were strictly applied in our history, Ylongo should be the basis of our proposed national language. It is the offspring of the ancient Hiniray-a (or Kinaray-a), the language brought by Datu Sumacuel and his companion-Bornean datus to the ten "Pulo sang Madia-as" or "Aninipay." Hiligaynon and Hinaray-a are the other names of modern Ylongo. The epic *Maragtas of Panay* tells us that, from Madia-as Aninipay, the old name of the heart-shaped island, the Malayan datus from Borneo spread to the four corners of our archipelago to form the other ethnic and language groups known, after the impact of Hispanic, as Filipinos.

The Sumacuel immigration to Panay was, perhaps, the most significant migrational wave of Malayans (Austronesians today) to our islands. With it came a defined, organized, and nearly literate culture, which is possibly today's silent foundation of our indigenousness. The Hiniray-a language brought by Sumacuel and his datus served as an agglutinative, an axis of approximation for our tongues in the past, when the Aeta and the Indonesian were probably the most vital heterogeneous elements in them.

Guillermo Gómez Rivera, "Prince of Ylongo Poetry."

When the Hiniray-a came in contact with Madia-as' tongue as Aninipay, Ylongo (Ilongo) or Hiligaynon evolved. When the Hiniray-a came in contact with the other pre-Malayan aborigines we had on the other islands, different dialects were born. The isolation from one another, which the datus and their respective descendants underwent after they parted ways from Panay Island, further explains the similarity and disparity of our indigenous tongues and cultures. Tagalogs, Ilocanos, Aclanenses, and Maguindanao Lumads are similar in tongue and culture. They share a common mother tongue, which many local linguists have described as "an ancient Malayo-Indo-Polynesian language."

However, let us analyze our various vernaculars. This ancient common Filipino tongue might be what is now known as the Hiniray-a or Kinaray-a vernacular of Antique and Central Panay. However, Tagalog was chosen as the basis of our proposed national language because the Spanish conquistadores made Manila, some four hundred years after Sumacuel, the capital of this archipelago.

Furthermore, if we follow the Spanish historical design, it is because the Spaniards continued the unification of our people started by the ten datus of Panay. The inchoate nationhood started by the Bornean datus also explains why Spanish became a stronger agglutinative after three hundred thirty-three years of Spanish rule. It is a fresher axis of unity for our vernacular tongues. To eliminate its influence from our dialects, as the Tagalog puristas are bent on doing, is to shatter the axis which gives our vernaculars a sense of homogeneity in their present form.

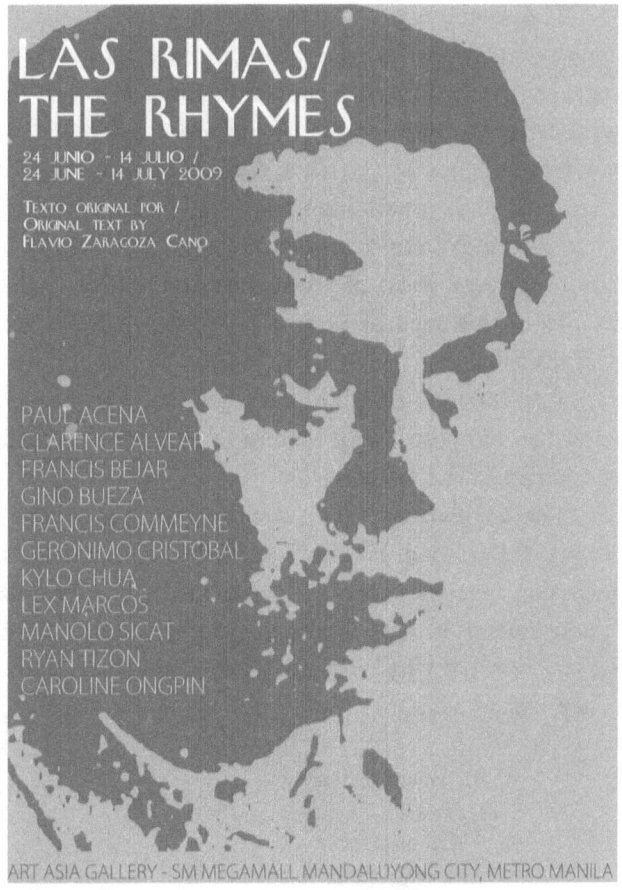

This poster promotes an art exhibition that features excerpts from the poetry of Flavio Zaragoza Cano as its textual content.

Aside from these known facts, Ylongo, the term now used to mean both the Hiniray-a and the Hiligaynon tongues of Panay-Aninipay, registers in the folds of its etymology, lexical structure, philology, and syntax the hidden chapters of our pre-Spanish history. It also records in its oral and written literature, particularly in poetry, the inquietudes of the races that have embraced it as their mother tongue.

In context, Ylongo poetry is predominantly indigenous. In form, measure and accentuation, it is purely Spanish. The contemporary Ylongo poet is the only vernacular writer who composes verses with perfect Spanish rhyme. He also applies the rigid classical Castilian accentuation or meter. These rules have placed Ylongo poetry on a higher plane than poetry in the other vernaculars.

The beginnings of verse-making among the Ylongos are marked by the appearance of old ballads which narrate the world's creation, the miracles (history) of Panay-Aninipay before Spain, and other historical events. These epics were never written. They became oral traditions, which later gave way to the corridos antiguos of the *Don Juan Tiñoso* school, which, aside from being sung, were printed in small librettos. The meter of these old songs is irregular. The verse oscillates from octosyllable (eight syllables) to hendecasyllable (eleven syllables). However, most of them were written along the verso romance. Introduced by Spain, this type of verse is octosyllable, with accentuations on the third and seventh syllables.

The corridos antiguos later gave way to the corridos modernos, popularly known as composos, with themes lifted from true-to-life experiences, ranging from the jocose to the tragic.

The popularity of the composo lasted up to the "Liberation," the years following the Second World War. Before the Liberation, the mass media—radio, television, and newspapers—were not yet fully established in the Philippines. These composos were produced according to the meter prescribed for the Spanish sextas, and they had six syllables, a standard beginning, and a typical ending. They began:

    O, manga Señores   Hear ye, Gentlemen,
    Pamati-i ninyo.   For I will sing
    Ako maga-asoy   A minor ballad.
    Diotay ñga composo,   Town of.......
    Banwa sang.......   There happened
    May natabu didto   Between four brothers
    Apat ka mag-utod   All of them halfbreeds.
    Puro guid mestizo.

    Pananglit may sayop   If there be any mistake
    Inyong dispensaron   In the narrative
    Bag-o lang mag-alam   Please pardon me
    Sining verso nakon...   For I have just learned
                                   These verses.

An example of satire and criticism are the following composo verses:

    Ining pagtulon-an   This new education
    Madamo'ng gadayaw,   Is praised by many
    Lalake, babae   The man and the woman
    Nagakuyawyaw   Are all in a hurry,
    Kon sila maghinambal   When they speak

Puro guid sing Inglés	It's all English
Gali kon sayuron	And all they mean
Kay enamores.	Is love making
Sa hagdan makadto	If I will go
Gali kon sayuron	To the stairs she goes
Si inday malagyo.	All this means
	That missy is eloping.

Together with the composo moderno, the couplet, known as coplas in the vernacular, appeared. Most popular of this genre was the "Si Inday" series, a set of descriptive verses exalting the native beauties through a sing-song melody familiar to Ylongos.

Si Inday ñga maitum-itum	The Miss that is blackie-blackie
Añgay guid sa balay ñga butóng,	Is fit to live in a bamboo hut.
Kon siá ang magyuhum-yuhum,	When she goes a smiley-smiley
Daw búlak sang cachubong.	She's the Trumpet flower.
Si Inday ñga mapula-pula	The Miss that is reddish-reddish
Añgay guid sa casa nga naga.	Is fit to live in a wooden house
Kon siá maggawagawa,	She's like the flower Impatient Balsamina
Daw búlak sang tapulañga.	When she looks out the window.

What is interesting about these composos and coplas is that their authors are unknown. People made them for their enjoyment and delight. However, this is just one aspect of Ylongo poetry.

※

VERSE-MAKING ALSO related to the moro-moros, the zarzuelas, and the comedias, which simultaneously enjoyed a revival during the Japanese Occupation, only to be forgotten with the advent of movies. The importance of these moro-moros, comedias, and zarzuelas regarding poetry is that they brought to the limelight the names of the personalities that can now be called the pioneers of Ylongo poetry. To this generation of dramatists and verse-makers belonged Angel Magahum, Eriberto Gumbán, and Valentín Cristóbal. Their verses remain popular among the older generations who watched their stage plays. However, these works have virtually been tossed into oblivion among the younger generations.

After these pioneers came the golden era of Ylongo poetry. With the verses of Flavio Zaragosa Cano, Delfín Gumbán, Magdalena Jalandoni, and Serapión C. Torre, poetry was a serious medium for the political, economic, romantic, and cul-

The giants of Ylongo literature: Magdalena Jalandoni, Delfín Gumbán, and Flavio Zaragosa Cano.

tural education of the masses. The poets in Hiligaynon were also poets in Spanish, and this particular bilingualism further enriched the vernacular literature.

Zaragosa Cano was thrice crowned "Principe Sang Mañga Poeta sa Ylongo." A political figure, labor leader, and nationalist newspaperman, he was feared by the American empire builders. However, his political and cultural ideas were more articulate in the Castilian tongue. He gave his lyricism to Ylongo while unleashing in ardent Spanish verses the gratitude of the Filipino to Spain and the fatal effects of the American intrusion into the Filipino soul. He was a prolific poet in both idioms. His Ylongo verses were dressed with colorful Latin metaphors, and his inspiration ranged from the erotic to the religious. Zaragosa's poetic accentuation, or meter, is so perfect in Hiligaynon, which makes his poems beautiful music to the ear.

"Halad Kay San Roque" is a model in hendecasyllable accentuation, classified under Spanish poetry as verso de arte mayor. Stresses are usually on the sixth and tenth syllables, if not over the fourth, the eighth, and the tenth.

> Guinpili ka sang Diwa ñga bala-an
> Ñga mañgin bulóng sang amon kasakitan,
> Kay ikaw ang dalangpan ñga duma-an
> Sa balati-an ñga labing dalitan.
> O mahal ñga San Roque, and imo ñgalan
> Tima-an sang kalu-oy ñga hamili
> Kay bisan gani sa tuñga sang dálan,
> Ang gugma nimo wala sing kapili.

The difference between a verse of arte mayor and that of arte menor lies in the number of syllables a verse may have. All verses with less than nine syllables

THE INDEPENDENT HISTORY OF YLONGO AND CEBUANO VISAYANS 171

fall under arte menor. Those with nine or more syllables are classified as versos de arte mayor. But Zaragoza Cano is also a master in arte menor.

Ang bulan sang Mayo	The month of May
Bulan sang sinadya	Is the month of happiness.
Among pagsaulog	It is when we adore
Kay Virgen María.	The Virgin Mary.
May mga pagdayaw	There are praises
Nga labing toto-o	Which are very sincere
Sa ngalan sang Iloy	In the name of the Mother
Sang aton Guino-o	Of our Lord.

...

Sa mata may luha,	She has tears in her eyes.
May paghinulsol;	There is remorse.
Asawang batan-on	The young wife feels
Daw sa may pagbasol.	Like blaming herself.
Sa labing pagsunggod,	Because of a big disappointment,
Na pílas ang dughan.	Her heart was wounded.
Gahulat ñga tamdon	She yearns to be minded.
Kag ulo-ulohan.	And to be wooed.

Zaragoza Cano was one of a famed "Trinidad Poética Ylonga." The other two were Serapión C. Torre and Delfín Gumbán.

A delegate from Agusan to the 1934 Constitutional Convention, a lawyer, former judge, and Spanish professor, Gumbán was named Ylongo poet laureate. His poetry is philosophical and patriotic. His "Subá Ang Kinabuhi," influenced by the Spanish medieval poet Jorge Manrique, can stand as a classic in vernacular poetry.

Suba ang kabuhi.	Life is like a river.
Nagailog wa-ay lañgan kag padayon	It flows without stopping.
Sa lawud sang kamatayon...	It continues
Wala sa gahum kag manggad.	To the sea which is death...
Mag-alañgay ang binilog.	There is no power nor wealth.
Halangdon kag pinanambi,	Everything is equal to it.
bata, lampong kag tigúlang —	The honorable and the outcast,
Wala sing kapin kag kulang.	the young, the adolescent, and the old —
Ang madalum kag manabaw,	No more. No less.
ang mainit kag masulog,	The river that is deep, that is shallow,
Sa dagat tanan madulog.	that is slow and overflowing.
Ang gamhanan kag timawa	All end up in the sea.
sa lulubñgan magadulog,	The powerful and the powerless
Di-in ang manga tanda-an	in the grave will sleep,
sang kahimtañgan mapanas,	Where all personal honors will be erased

Katulad sang manga pangpang	Like the ebbing and eroding
sang suba ñga nagalanas!	banks of a river.

The Spanish octosílabo, when applied to Ylongo poetry, takes on unsuspected might. His "Ambahan sa Kaluwasan" (Song to Liberty) was given a prize for being a perfect poem of patriotic inspiration in Visayan. The poet deplores America's land-grabbing tactics. He calls America's former plan to grant us independence if we ceded to it the island of Mindanao "a diabolical amputation of Filipino patrimony." Of course, the plan was not carried out, but here are the verses to commemorate the intention. This poem was written on May 2, 1926.

Kon ang palad nian kabós	If luck is now lacking
apang may kalag ñga lagting	There are strong spirits
ñga gala-um ñga magbagting	Who are waiting for the bell
ang ágong sang pagtubos	of liberty to sound
sa banwa ko ñga kubós	their freedom.
ang langit ñga malahalon	The majestic skies
sa iya kalag nagpabalon	have given my humble
sing ma-init ñga pagtu-o	people ardent faith,
ñga sa Diwang kamumu-o	embedded in the spirit,
wa'y talikalang salsalon!	faith in justice, faith in the fact
Dili na ang banwa magpati	that in God's hands
sa America kag magtu-o	there are no iron chains.
sa panug-an ñga nalu-o	My people don't believe
ñga bu-ot sa aton ikati;	in America anymore.
dapat ñga ang salampati	They have lost faith in stale promises
mañgaman sa Saligyawan	The dove of peace should beware
ñga wala sing ka-ayawan	because there is no foreign
kag guinahañgad sa duta,	power that can be satisfied,
kundi pagbusog, pagbuta	in this earth with anything less
sang kahakug sing bulawan.	than power, wealth
	and abundant gold.

Instead of Torre's poems, which are unavailable at the moment, we have Magdalena Jalandoni's "Ang Guitarra," an ode to that instrument of love and nostalgia, which according to Gumbán, is enough to consecrate Miss Jalandoni as the lyric poet of the country. Doña Magdalena, a Jareña through and through, belongs to the same era which produced Zaragoza Cano and Gumbán. She has read a lot in Spanish and was educated in Spanish, but hardly wrote in this language, as her male counterparts did She has, nevertheless, a superb mastery of Spanish

The coplas of Spanish poet Jorge Manrique have a great influence on Ylongo poetry.

meter. Let "Ang Guitarra" speak for this Parnassian poet. Note the fourteen syllables of the "Alejandrino," reminiscent of Rizal's "Mi Ultimo Adios" meter. This type of poetic form is distinguished by the caesura, also common in Tagalog poetry, after every seven syllables.

Ang baw-ing ñga manga dalan	The winding streets, when
kon hadkan kag pasili-on	kissed and lighted by the
Sang bulan ñga naga-ugsad	gazing moon, which has
kag nañgin añgay sa sulu.	converted itself into a
Upod sa kúlas sang hangin	lamp together with the
ñga hálus gani bati-on	blowing wind which can
Ang guitarra nagabuylog	hardly be heard, the guitar
sa hinay ñga hilibi-on	helps the faint cries
Sa pagsuguid sang kasakit	of a heart which is
Ñga una niyang guinmulu.	speaking of the pain
Halin sa patag kag bukid	which it once felt.
ñga sang bulan napawa-an	From the plains and mountains
Halin sa payag nga diotay	illumined by the moon
Ñga daw guinbuksan sing huñgod,	From the small hut where doors
Pamati-i kay galanton ang guitarrañga duma-an,	and windows have been opened,
Pamati-i kay gatu-aw ang nahut niyang bala-an	Listen, because the old guitar is playing,
Sang panaghoy ñga sa gugma	Listen, because its holy strings speak
Kag sa kamiñgaw natuñgod.	of a sigh, of a cry,
Kag ayhan sa kasingkasing	begotten of love and loneliness.
sang gakuskos ñga tag-iya	And perhaps in the heart
May tunay ñga kasulub-on	of the strummer
ñga dili didto makakas,	There exists a natural romanticism
Kay samtang nagalanton	which cannot be uprooted,
ang tagsa ka nahut niya	Because while every string vibrates
Wala sing dili mawili sa pagpamati sa iya,	Nobody can't help but be delighted to listen,
Wala sing dili bumatyag	Nobody can't help but express
sing kasulub-on ñga lakás.	a long-hidden sadness.

Ylongo poetry is one of most important treasures of our spiritual patrimony as a people. The poets of this vernacular talk about all the aspects of daily life. What a pity, however, that with the decline of Castilian in our country, Ylongo poetry has suffered.

The old poets of the Hispanic school hardly have any literary descendants. With the advent of free verse in Hiligaynon, under the new culture's influence, the quality, from form to context, of the poetry produced in this vernacular today has become very poor.

To remedy this situation, our new vernacular poets should master the Spanish meter and the Spanish language itself.

CHAPTER XIV
PRICELESS CHILDHOOD MEMORIES RECALLED

The Tabugón Barrio School was where we attended classes after our arrival in Iloilo from Manila following the end of the Second World War in 1945. Our biological mother, Lourdes Rivera y Celo, was with us during the move, and our adopted mother, Rosa Jiménez Gayoso de Rivera, was overjoyed to have us back. We stayed with Mama Rosita and her husband, José Rivera, our maternal grandfather, in Barrio Tabugón, Municipio de Dingle, Provincia de Iloilo. Abuelito José resumed working on his sugarcane hacienda to save money for building a two-story house on the property of Mama Rosita on Calle Bonifacio in Iloilo City.

In many ways, Iloilo was still recovering from the devastation of the war, and the Japanese had just left the country. At nine years old, we needed to catch up with our elementary education. Our mother, Lourdes, went back to Manila to search for work, and our father, Francisco, went to see if they could reconcile after their long separation.

During the war, the old Tabugón ancestral house of the Rivera family was burned down by the USAFFE (United States Army Forces Far East) to prevent its use by the Japanese, who never came to Tabugón.

As we attended the Tabugón public elementary school, Mama Rosita continued to make us read in Spanish. Our children's workbook was called a catón (primer or first reading book). After mastering it, we began reading novels, poetry, and current events from two Visayan weeklies published in Iloilo City—*Yuhum* (Smile) and *Kasanag* (Light).

Our English was poor, but it was at a much better level than our Tabugón elementary schoolmates, who hardly knew

Front row, from left: José Yreñeta, Henry Miller, and the author's father, Francisco "Paco" Gómez. Standing from left: Guillermo Lanza and Federico González.

it. They all pretended to understand when the male principal and the two female teachers spoke. In the end, to understand one another, everybody had to revert

Guillermo with his Tita Concejo (standing, left), his mother Lourdes and his adopted mother, Rosa Jiménes Gayoso de Rivera (seated). The young boy is Anthony Miller, his cousin and son of Concejo.

to the vernacular, Quinaray-a, which we also mastered since it was different from the vernacular of the city.

We had many pet dogs at home. We ran over the rice fields and swam in the nearby Jalaud River, and we would occasionally hike and swim in the springs of Moroboro.

Every Sunday, we would all attend Mass at the Dingle Roman Catholic Church, which was five kilometers away from our Barrio Tabugón. Over time we got to know everybody in Dingle, like the Monteros, the Dalipes, the Dayots, the Roceses, and the Hernández Gaviras, who were all Spanish-speaking. Most of the other children we knew lived in fear and fascination with the local sorcerer they called "asuang," Teniente Guimó, whom we later wrote about in our first novel in Spanish, *Quis ut Deus, el brujo rebelde de Yloilo*. We frequented the town fiestas of Dingle, Dueñas, Pototan, and Passi, where we would play panguingue as the partner (sangga) of our Mama Rosita, who loved that old card game. During these fiestas, Mama Rosita would also make us dance flamenco and sing the many Mexican songs she taught us in Spanish. In the meantime, everybody would stop playing madiong and panguingue to clap and cheer in Visayan while throwing peso bills at us from their game tables. We, the group of children from our barrio, were taught how to sing popular American songs by a piano teacher from the nearby town of Pototan. Among the songs we learned were "Make Believe," "Some Sunday Morning," "You Are My Sunshine," "Moonlight Bay," "Indian Love Call," "It Had to Be You," "Stardust," and "Somewhere Over the Rainbow."

Our barrio school principal, Mister Perono, soon discovered our singing abilities and made us perform during the early flag ceremony every Monday morning in the barrio school for all to hear. He would lead us in singing the American national anthem, followed by the Filipino national anthem in English. Despite there being no radio station reaching our barrio at that time, we enjoyed singing and showing off our skills to the community.

Guillermo Gómez Rivera and his flamenco dance partner Nelia Jaruda Jocson performed together when he was in his younger years.

Our grandfather had fought for Spain as an Ylongo Voluntario before joining the Aguinaldo army of the República de Filipinas to fight the American invaders of Iloilo, led by General Marcus P. Miller. He asked his wife, Mama Rosita, to teach us how to sing the Filipino hymn in Spanish.

Later, our grandfather approached Mister Perono and asked if we could perform the hymn in its original Spanish version during the weekly flag ceremony. However, much to our grandfather's chagrin, the principal politely refused.

Fortunately, Mama Rosita had a solution. She suggested that we perform popular English songs and their Spanish versions during the flag ceremony instead. These included "Solamente una vez" ("You Belong to My Heart") and "Siempre en mi corazón" ("You Are Always in My Heart").

AT THIS TIME, our grandfather's youngest daughter, Concejo, also known as Tita Connie to us, tied the knot with Henry Miller, the son of Joseph Miller. Joseph was rumored to be the son of General Miller. Joseph, who arrived in the Philippines with his alleged father on the same warship, the *USS Petrel*, attained the rank of captain in the U.S. Navy but decided to settle in Iloilo where he married a local woman from Barrio Jaguimit in Dueñas, Iloilo province. Tito Henry and

The photograph shows Joseph Miller with his children, including his only son Henry whom he is holding. Henry later married the author's aunt, Concejo.

Tita Connie, along with their daughters Rosemarie and Jean Louise, came to live with us as part of the Rivera family in Tabugón. Like his father, Tito Henry had become fluent in Spanish due to the influence of their wives.

After the Philippine-American War (1899-1902), Joseph retired from the U.S. military. With his Filipina wife from Dueñas, six kilometers from Tabugón, he used his retirement money to build a stone mansion in Barrio Jaguimit, whose ruins can still be seen today. He had five children; Henry was his only son. Joseph often expressed regret over the U.S. bombardment of Iloilo City in 1899. He became a member of America's Anti-Imperialist League, founded in 1898 by famous Americans, including Mark Twain, who opposed the annexation of the Philippines. Despite his sentiments after the war, Joseph expected the Philippines to eventually become a state of the United States, which did not happen. He lived contentedly and is buried in the American Cemetery by Calle Comisión Civil in Jaro, Iloilo. He was a friend of our Gómez-Windham grandfather (Felipe) and our granduncle (Guillermo), whom he said were also Americans of British extraction but rooted in Massachusetts, U.S.A.

Our adopted mother, Mama Rosita, taught us to be proud of our British American mestizo heritage, as no one can choose their ancestors. She also stressed the importance of appreciating our native Filipino roots and our Spanish and Chinese lineage. Moreover, she emphasized that we are native-born Filipinos raised as

Ilustrados and have a moral duty to serve and defend our country. She also taught us to love Spain as it is our Mother Country.

Another friend of Joseph Miller was an American investor, Mr. Thomas Ford, who married a local Spanish mestiza, María Garcia. Thomas also spoke Spanish with a heavy American accent and was close to our maternal grandfather, José Rivera, whom he called "Peipeeto." He and María Garcia Ford owned the sugarcane mill at Dumalág, Capiz, where our grandfather Pepito milled his sugarcane. In addition to the two hundred hectares of land our grandfather owned, he leased twenty-five hectares of Tabugón sugarland held by Mrs. María Ford. While we were still babies, the Fords and Joseph visited our house in Tabugón, and Joseph even planted sugarcane in his hacienda in Barrio Jaguimit, Dueñas. He also used the Ford-Garcia sugarcane mill in Capiz, then connected to Tabugón by the Philippine Railways Company.

While completing our studies at the University of San Agustín in Iloilo, we gained a reputation as an outstanding Spanish dance instructor, a *Halintang sa Kadungganan* champion, a radio singer, and a talented Visayan Ylongo poet and writer. We were even honored with welcome banners in Guimarás Island during the annual Good Friday ("Ang Pagtaltal") reenactment of Christ's passion and resurrection, where we were hailed as the "Prince of Hiligaynon Poetry." Aquilino "Quiling" Secusana, a former high school classmate of ours at San Agustín, organized the festival. Meanwhile, Señor Ui, a Spanish-speaking principal at Sun Yat Sen High School in Iloilo, happily employed us to teach parián Spanish danc-

The rusted railway tracks, once maintained by the now-defunct Philippine Railways Company, lay abandoned with an obsolete train stranded on them. The sugarcane growers relied heavily on the railway for transporting their sugarcane harvest from the farms to the sugar mill.

es and Tagalog at the prestigious Chinese school. These were busy and lucrative times for this writer in the 1950s.

Our childhood in Tabugón left an indelible imprint on our souls that would continue to shape us as we began a new chapter of our lives in Iloilo City. We would go on to open more chapters of our lives as young men in Manila, where we eventually settled permanently, but we would never forget our golden roots in Iloilo City and province, and even our origins in Negros Occidental.

The remnants of the Miller mansion can be found in Barangay Jaguimit, Dueñas, Iloilo.

The author is seated between his first cousins, Joseph Miller and Jean Louise Miller. Their mother, Concejo, who has since passed away, was married to a man who is thought to be a grandson of Brigadier General Marcus P. Miller. The general is remembered for leading the assault on Iloilo at the start of the Philippine-American War (1899-1902), which eventually resulted in the city's capture by the American forces.

CHAPTER XXV
THE HISPANIC CULTURE OF CEBU

In our adolescent years, our adoptive mother Rosita enlisted her husband José to build a two-story house on a plot of land spanning over a thousand square meters. This land was inherited from Mama Rosita's ancestors and was located on Bonifacio Street. The property was situated across from a vast park with the provincial jail on its left and the winding Iloilo River on its right. In the far distance on the right-hand side stood the majestic Casa Real or Casa Gobierno, a grand old building from the Spanish era that has since been restored. It overlooks the site where the Arroyo fountain stands, which marks the start of the long and broad Calle Iznart. This street connects to the circular Plazoleta Gay, from which Iloilo's historic Calle Real, the city's central street, originates. Calle Real snakes leisurely before ending at the lush Plaza Libertad, after which it fades southward toward the Iloilo Strait.

The land where the old Casa Gobierno stood, along with the surrounding neighborhoods of Calles Iznart, Luna, Valeria, Muelle Loney, Joveler, Solis, Fuentes, and Delgado, were initially owned by the Gayoso-Jiménez clan, led by Victoriano Gayoso and Diego Jiménez Frades. Several of these historic streets intersect or culminate at Calle Ledesma, which divides old Iloilo in half and nearly reaches the Tanza seashore where the ancient cemetery is located.

The Gayoso-Jiménez mansion still stands today and is part of the Doane complex owned by Protestants. It is located next to Mama Rosita's old property, which now belongs to the Jardelezas and is part of the same old residential line as the Don Eusebio Villanueva mansion. Several Ledesma mansions follow the Gayoso-Jiménez mansion in the row, ending at the Ledesma Hotel, which is near the Tabucan Bridge leading to La Paz and Jaro. I was adopted by Mama Rosita, who was the daughter of Don Diego Jiménez Frades, the publisher and writer of *El Porvenir de Visayas*. Her mother was a Gayoso heiress. Interestingly, I am the legal grandson of Don Diego of the defunct *El Porvenir de Visayas*.

The mention of Diego Jiménez Frades and his publication revives the memory of Iloilo's Spanish Creole roots and its era of growth, wealth, joy, sophistication, grandeur, charm, and bliss. Vintage photographs depict elegantly attired women and children heading to fairs, festivals, carnivals, and civic-military processions linked to the esteemed Casino Español de Iloilo. The composition of Iloilo and its surroundings is comparable to that of Cebu.

The founders and builders of Cebu had a vision for the city's future based on its diverse population. The pragmatic Spanish conquistadores recognized that three dominant ethnic groups would shape the city: the indigenous community

Captured in Time: Life in Cebu's Old Parián district from perhaps the early twentieth century, showcasing a vastly different pace of life compared to the bustling metropolis of present-day.

led by its principalía de indios, the chinos cristianos or Chinese Sangleys, and the criollos and mestizos.

Similarly, the development of Metro Iloilo began when the Spanish authorities expanded the original Villa de Arévalo settlement, including the Plaza Libertad swamps with streets like Rosario and Durán. They also developed lots that extended to the Sunburst Park area, including streets like Ortiz and Mapa, all the way down to the seashore, creating what is now known as Ciudad Española.

Local history suggests that the notion of a Ciudad Española in Iloilo was derived from a wealthy Spanish gentleman, whose last name was Ledesma. The said individual possessed a significant portion of the city and its neighboring districts. As the story goes, he wedded three successive china cristiana ladies and fathered a brood of offspring and descendants, some of whom still have a presence in the city to this day. It remains uncertain why, but either Ledesma himself or one of his descendants chose to legally isolate their grand abode in the Ciudad Española from the rest of the family lots.

The thriving and affluent Creole Spanish community of Iloilo had a magnificent second-floor venue for their Casino Español, which occupied the old Jepte-Sáenz Building next to the now-demolished Eagle Theatre. Given that all the residents were Spanish subjects or citizens, several of the casino's founders, including those of chino cristiano or indio principalía ancestry, such as Don Serafín Villanueva, Emiliano Lizares, and Manuel Marquez-Lim, were also involved in its establishment. This is why the Ylongo mestrería was also active in the carnival dances and shows of Iloilo, Jaro, and even far-flung municipalities such as Passi, which is now a city.

※

THE ARRIVAL OF Salvador Rueda, the Spanish poet laureate, in 1915 left a lasting impression on the city of Iloilo. The organizers went to great lengths to involve the city's population in the festivities, and the group photograph of the reception and records they left behind testify to the unity and efficient organization of the Ylongos. However, this sense of unity and cohesion began to decline in the first few decades of the 1900s, as an American communist-influenced political movement took hold and led to the city's economic, social, and cultural decline. The Ylongo Voluntarios attributed the unnecessary destruction of the Ylongo economy to the colonialist American government and its secret agencies, committed to destroying the established Filipino-Hispano Ilustrado order. The government's Masonic Worcester-Santos Abakada purista language policy and ideology endures as the remaining centerpiece of that movement, which has caused extensive damage as evident in the increasing illiteracy rate in the country.

The photograph of the 1915 reception for Rueda in Iloilo City shows insight into the peaceful, economically stable, and prosperous society governed by a conservative and progressive Hispanic Christian-Catholic culture, nurtured by the Spanish-speaking Voluntario forces of 1900 in Iloilo City and province. Manila's Binondo is promoted as "the world's oldest Chinatown," despite it being established as an "encomienda y pueblo" by Spaniards in the fifteenth century. However, the area commonly referred to as "Chinatown" is actually the old Parián or Binondo Sector de Mestizos. The label of "world's oldest Chinatown" is simply a tourism ploy, and it is possible that the parianes in Cebu and Iloilo are much older than Binondo.

The term parián has even made its way to Mexican cities in reference to Chinese trade via Manila. Still, very few people in Manila today understand why due to the loss of Spanish influence and American intrusion and prejudice. Even today, there is anti-Spanish prejudice in the Philippines, which can be attributed to the backward Abakada purista language and culture policy enforced by Philippine education in the 1900s and 1930s. On the flip side, many crucial remnants of Cebu's past, particularly those of the old Parián, have slowly vanished, causing harm to the development of a higher and more complete Cebuano identity. Therefore, urgent actions are needed to address this progressive decay of the Hispanic-Oceanian identity.

THE INDEPENDENT HISTORY OF YLONGO AND CEBUANO VISAYANS

A BOOK TITLED *Life in Old Parian* (Cebuano Studies Center, University of San Carlos, 1983) by Concepción Gantuangco Briones was published as an important step to preserve Cebuano history. The book was meticulously researched and documented, with an introduction by historian Resil B. Mojares, director of the Cebuano Studies Center at San Carlos University.

Briones' book begins with a heartbreaking claim that the Cebu Parián, along with other historical areas of Cebu City, was burned down by the USAFFE in 1942, a few days before the Japanese invasion. According to Briones, the heartland of Parián, Colon Street, and various parts of downtown Cebu City were completely destroyed to deny the incoming Japanese forces a place to stay. However,

This vintage photograph likely taken in the early 1900s shows chino cristiano shoemakers vending their products at the Old Parián in Cebu.

this explanation is deemed insufficient since the Japanese soldiers still found other buildings to use, and they established their camp in Cebu. The USAFFE was not "departing," but fleeing in fear from the Japanese. The intentional destruction of Parián was an attempt to erase Cebuano history, which had Spanish and Chinese roots and was thus considered an obstacle to the "Americanization plan" for future generations of Filipinos who were to be taught only in English, Taglish, or Cebuglish. This desire to erase the past was part of the Americanization agenda.

It should be noted that while the "Americanization agenda" continues to exist to some degree, it has been curbed, possibly out of shame, as its aim of removing Hispanic influence has already been achieved to a certain extent. However, recent experts have discovered the severity of this colonial agenda, which has had a significant impact on the reading abilities of Filipino students in elementary and high school, resulting in concern among WB and IMF monitors about the rising functional illiteracy among Filipinos. This decline in basic literacy and cultural development can be traced back to the 1950s and has had a detrimental impact on the Filipino people. As a result, there are now advocates who dedicate their time, effort, and resources to preserving their shared heritage.

Fortunately, Cebu Parián has produced a champion in the form of Valentino M. Sandiego, who, together with his wife Ofelia Zozobrado, has become a prominent cultural figure representing modern Parián de Cebu in various cultural activities, including the Sinulog Festival. Val and Ofelia, who are highly skilled in dance, choreography, music, culture, and design, have also inherited the oldest surviving Parián house in Cebu City and the province, ingeniously transforming it into a highly regarded museum that is of significant importance to the country's tourism, education, and history. In addition, they operate a ballet and dance studio to nurture aspiring young Cebuano dance artists. Val and Ofelia also lead a Sinulog dance group that adds tremendous energy and vibrancy to the city's annual festival in honor of the widely revered Santo Niño de Cebu. A pamphlet that has been widely distributed states:

A book titled "Life in Old Parian" by Concepción Gantuangco Briones was published as an important step to preserve Cebuano history. The book was meticulously researched and documented.

The Yap-Sandiego Ancestral House is located at 155 Lopez-Jaena corner Mabini Street in Cebu's Parián. Considered to be the oldest residential house in the Philippines, it was built between 1675 and 1700 by a Chinese merchant named Don Juan Yap and his wife, Doña María Florido del Mar. They had three children, María, Eleuterio, and Consolación. During the 1880s, María married Don Mariano Sandiego from Obando, Bulacan, who was the Cabeza de Barangay of the Cebu Parián. A few years ago, the great-great-grandson of Doña María, Val Sandiego, known in Cebu as an art collector, choreographer, and heritage icon, turned over this house. Under his care, he restored the ancestral house and turned it into the famous museum and tourist attraction it is today. It showcases artworks, life-size statues like the Santo Niño, and antique furniture made of Philippine wood like balayong, molave, and narra. With the knowledge this house offers, we will begin to truly understand how we became what we are today.

Val is the son of Luz Mancao, a Physical Education teacher from a landed family in Carcar. This town is situated in the southern part of Cebu province and is renowned for its Hispanic ancestral homes, as well as the Arabesque-Andalusian style of the Santa Catalina Parish Church. The majority of landowners

The Yap-Sandiego Ancestral House, located in Cebu's historic old Parián district, offers visitors a unique opportunity to step back in time and experience the grandeur of a bygone era. This ancestral house is a testament to the opulence of the wealthy Filipino families of the eighteenth century.

in Carcar are chino cristiano and Spanish mestizo families who originally lived in the ancient Cebu Parián.

As you enter the Yap-Sandiego Ancestral House, you'll be greeted by a grand foyer adorned with priceless treasures, such as antique furniture and intricate artworks. The walls are lined with portraits of the family's ancestors, providing a glimpse into their rich heritage. The house boasts an impressive collection of artifacts and historical memorabilia, each with its own story to tell.

One of the most striking features of the Yap-Sandiego Ancestral House is its architecture. The structure itself is a marvel of traditional Filipino architecture, with its sturdy coral stone walls and intricate wooden carvings. The house has stood the test of time and has survived earthquakes and typhoons, making it a testament to the durability of traditional Filipino design.

Exploring the different rooms of the ancestral house, visitors can gain a deeper understanding of the customs, beliefs, and lifestyles of the Yap and Sandiego families. The kitchen, for example, is a fascinating space that showcases the culinary traditions of the era, with antique cooking implements and utensils on display. The bedrooms, on the other hand, are a glimpse into the family's private lives, with intricately designed beds and wardrobes that give visitors a sense of the family's style and taste.

The Yap-Sandiego Ancestral House is not just a museum, but a living embodiment of Cebu's cultural heritage. It provides a unique opportunity for visitors to experience the richness of Filipino history, and serves as a reminder of the importance of preserving our past for future generations. Whether you're a history buff or simply curious about the past, a visit to the Yap-Sandiego Ancestral House is sure to be a memorable and enlightening experience.

In the book *Life in Old Parian*, it is stated that the majority of Chinese and mestizo Spanish families in the Parián area also owned vast expanses of land such as haciendas, arrozales, and maizales in Carcar and other municipalities in Cebu, Leyte, and Bohol. The Spanish authorities implemented a land distribution policy called encomienda, which prevented any Masonic revolutionary influence from infiltrating the elite of Visayas in the 1890s. Unlike the Rizal family who became tenants of friar lands in Laguna and joined the Katipunan Masons to seize already developed friar haciendas in southern Luzon, Cebuano and Ylongo landowners became Leales Voluntarios. They disavowed the Tagalog Katipunan Masons as ungrateful and traitorous to the European motherland.

Additionally, the affluent Chinese Christians of Cebu and Iloilo parianes contributed money to support the Leales and Voluntarios in defending Spain against the Tagalog Katipunan. They rightfully perceived the Katipunan as a progressive fifth column of spies working for the Americans who were coveting the remaining Spanish overseas territories in the Caribbean and the Pacific, including Filipinas.

Given this context, it is understandable why León Kilát, a Katipunero recruiter and rebel, was assassinated by Cebuanos. Despite this, the government in Manila insists on imposing upon unsuspecting Cebuano children the story of León Kilát, whom their forefathers collectively rejected along with the treacherous Katipunan. President Emilio Aguinaldo of the Primera República de Filipinas disbanded the Katipunan and ordered the execution of Andrés and Procopio Bonifacio in Mount Buntis, Cavite, for betraying the Filipino people.

※

IN 1971, PRESIDENT Ferdinand Marcos y Edralin Sr. called for a Constitutional Convention to draft a new constitution for the country. One of the changes made was replacing the coined Tagalog purista term "Pilipino" with "Filipino." This change was accompanied by the discontinuation of the Abakada and the Lope K. Santos purist Balarila-driven Tagalog, which represented a fabricated indigenous

Completed in the year 2000, the Plaza Parián in Cebu was a lengthy three-year project that displays a number of works of art created by Eduardo Castrillo. The art pieces portray several notable landmarks and symbols of Cebu, such as the Basilica Santo Niño, St. John the Baptist Church, a Spanish Galleon, the Cebu Metropolitan Cathedral, and the famous Magellan's Cross. Using a mix of concrete, brass, steel, and bronze, the sculpture is a fine example of the artist's craft. The idea for the Heritage of Cebu originated from Castrillo and then Cebu Mayor Alvin B. Garcia, with the project being funded by contributions from private individuals and organizations.

culture. A significant number of delegates came from remote areas of the country where Visayan or other native languages were spoken. Initially, they did not fully comprehend what "Pilipino" meant. Later, they found out that it was Tagalog with many invented "aghimuin" or Esperanto-like words, which even ordinary Tagalogs did not know or understand. As a result, they were infuriated and offended by being forced to draft the new constitution in a language they did not know instead of using English.

Cebuano and Mindanao delegates, including Gerardo Pepito, Marcelo Fernán, Julio Ozamiz, and Natalio Bacalso, were quick to discern the ploy to establish the Tagalog puristas as the new ruling elite of the country, which they saw as an ambitious minority group trying to colonize the Philippines. The delegates were outraged by this prospect. They also realized that the purista Tagalogs would impose "Pilipino" on non-Tagalogs and abolish the original Spanish-speaking Filipino State, which was championed by figures like Rizal, Aguinaldo, and Mabini and established in 1571 with Manila as its capital. The State founded in 1571 was the cornerstone of the modern-day Philippines, and the purista Tagalogs aimed to replace it with a communist Tagalog State.

There was a plan in place to replace the existing Spanish-speaking Filipino State with a communist "Pilipinas" governed by the Tagalog puristas. This revisionist movement aimed to make non-Tagalogs second-class citizens while portraying themselves as proletarian communists. Writer-historian Nick Joaquín satirized the supposed heroes of this movement, including Andrés Bonifacio, as marching in Marxist boots, even though they were traditionally known to wear bakya. Unfortunately, Cebuano leaders such as Pepito, Fernán, Ozamiz, and Bacalso foresaw the serious consequences of this movement, particularly for non-Tagalogs who made up the majority of the country. Bacalso, a prominent radio commentator in the Visayas and Mindanao, spoke out against the Tagalog Abakada puristas, warning of the danger they posed to the country. Bacalso, who produced Cebuano-language films, also predicted the downfall of Visayan movies, which ultimately occurred.

On the one hand, Professor Leopoldo Yabes of the University of the Philippines represented the Ilocanos who criticized the Tagalog puristas for diminishing the use of English in the nation. Conversely, the Muslims called for secession. Meanwhile, José María Sison, founder of the Communist Party of the Philippines, Senator Benigno S. Aquino, and Luis Taruc, a peasant leader, were among the extremists who collaborated in the countryside and universities to incite and mobilize students toward violent government takeover.

In contrast, students communist sympathizers spearheaded protests calling for the abolition of ROTC and Spanish and Filipino literature courses in universities, which were authored by distinguished personalities such as Vicente Sotto, Miguel Cuenco, and Enrique Magalona from Cebu and Iloilo. The communist-inspired students rejected basic military training and the teaching of Philippine history and nationalism from the original Spanish texts of figures like Mabini, Recto, Bernabé, Balmori, and Aguinaldo in schools. Instead, they promoted Hollywood, drugs, and Marxism.

❧

AS A DEFENDER of the conservative Sino-Parián culture, Cebuana writer Concepción Briones highlighted the intellectual achievements of Filipinos who spoke Castilian. Her book, *Life in Old Parian,* serves as a powerful defense of Cebu and its Hispanic parián identity.

> What is little known and almost forgotten during the Eighties, however, is that it was also in Cebu where a golden era of journalism and literature flowered in the second and third decades of the 1900s.

Explore a stunning diorama of the San Juan Bautista Parish Church, or Parián Church, inside the Museo Parián sa Sugbo—1730 Jesuit House. Although the church no longer stands, this remarkable display transports visitors back in time with its remarkable attention to detail and masterful artistry. This enchanting depiction serves as a testament to the rich history and cultural heritage of the iconic landmark.

Val M. Sandiego and his wife Ofelia Zozobrado Sandiego work together as custodians of the Yap-Sandiego Ancestral House, located in Cebu's Old Parián district. Through their tireless efforts in cultural preservation, this dedicated couple has played a crucial role in maintaining the rich Spanish legacy of the city. Thanks to their unwavering commitment, the house has been preserved in its original form, providing a glimpse into the history of this historic district.

A group of erudite and illustrious Cebuano and Visayan writers ushered in the birth of journalism in this part of the country at the beginning of this century. In fact on the shoulders of the youthful Don Sergio Osmeña, the favorite son of Cebu, fell the obligation to pioneer in journalism in this southern region. He was the publisher-editor of *El Nuevo Día*, a Spanish language daily in 1900. Before 1900, however, there were already publications, like *El Nacional* and *La Justicia*, which came out in 1899, and Spanish government officials like the editors of *Del Superior Gobierno* also authored Spanish language leaflets and handbills. And though Osmeña's *Nuevo Día* lived for only three years up to 1903, its three-year continuous existence helped immensely in kindling interest in journalism here in Cebu and the rest of the Visayas.

The late writer educator-Zobel awardee, Prof. José María del Mar, used to tell us newspaper folk that two of the most important men in our country joined Osmeña as "reporters" on the staff of his *El Nuevo Día*. They were Don Rafael Palma of Manila and Don Jaime C. de Veyra of Leyte.

A few years later, on August 5, 1910, Don Filemón Sotto, Don Vicente's brother, started publishing his *La Revolución*, a Spanish language daily that existed until 1942, the year of the outbreak of WWII. Del Mar wrote in this *Diario* for twelve consecutive years.

How about offering Spanish language and flamenco classes at Casa Gorordo in Cebu? It would be a wonderful opportunity to showcase the region's rich Hispanic legacy and provide visitors with a deeper understanding of Cebuano culture and traditions.

Briefly, for one year, Representative Isidro Vamenta published the *La Tribuna* in which Del Mar also wrote.

Don Maríano Cuenco, a lawyer from Carmen, Cebu, moved his residence and his family to Parián and founded the Cuenco newspaper dynasty which exists up to the present. After the elder Don Maríano passed away, his wife, Doña Remedios López Cuenco, turned publisher. Her publishing offices were housed on the ground floor of the Cuenco residence along Calle Colón, and she operated and managed the Imprenta Rosario.

Doña Remedios Cuenco's three sons were all writers, and they had inherited printer ink in their veins from their father. Don Maríano Jesus Cuenco, who became an illustrious governor, representative and senator, edited *El Precursor*, a Spanish Visayan newspaper. His elder brother, the then Padre José María Cuenco edited an all-Spanish weekly, *El Boletin Católico*. A third son, lawyer-legislator Don Miguel Cuenco, contributed articles in Spanish and English to the family's dailies and weekly. Considered a worthy successor to Don Maríano's *El Precursor* is the younger Cuenco son's English daily, *The Republic News*.

Like the two Sottos and the Cuencos, Don Vicente Rama, often known as the father of Cebu City's charter, was a lawyer and a legislator. Don Vicente edited his fearless Spanish-Visayan daily, *La Nueva Fuerza-Ang Bag-ong Kusog*. This bi-lingual newspaper existed until 1942, when WWII broke out, on Calle Espeleta, San Nicolás.

In the flowering of literature during that golden era, Cebuanos attracted national and international acclaim. This was also the era when Cebu's dashing and handsome playwright, Governor Buenaventura Rodriguez, would be hailed in Spain as "the Mark Twain of the Philippines." This would be the era in Cebu's literary history when another son, Senator Manuel C. Briones would be hailed in Spain and continental Europe as "another Demosthenes" because of his literary genius, his reasoning power, and logic on any given subject of interest.

These admirable luminaries in our literary firmament often wrote in two or three languages. For example, the late Senator Jesus María Cuenco wrote news items for the family's *Republic News* in English as he wrote news stories in Visayan and articles in Spanish. On the other hand, Senator Vicente Rama dictated his reports for *La Nueva Fuerza*, first in Visayan, then translated them into English. From there, he would write the final version in Spanish. Another tri-lingual lawyer-legislator, the bon vivant of Cebu's old Ciudad district, Representative Vicente Logarta, the editor of *El Debate*, often dictated his speeches and articles in simple Visayan then also had them translated into English from which he also finally wrote the Spanish version. Representative Vicente Logarta of Cebu's second district was a Manila newspaperman before he became a lawyer and later a legislator.

Over the years, the Zobel memorial award for outstanding articles, novels, and pieces in the Spanish language honored several Cebuano wielders of the pen. Among them were representative Manuel C. Briones for a speech in the legislature, Don Buenaventura Rodriguez, then a reporter for the *El Renacimiento*, for his novel *La Pugna*, Dr. Ines Villa Gonzalez for her doctoral thesis at the Universidad Central de Madrid entitled 'Filipinas en el camino de la cultura,' Prof. Antonio María Abad of Barili, Cebu, for his novel *El Campeón*, Don Vivente Padriga for his essay 'Obras Jóvenes' and Prof. José María del Mar for his 'Perfiles or profiles of such great Filipinos as Claro Mayo Recto, Rafael Palma, Fernando María Guerrero, Cecilio Apóstol and others.

Of the above Zobel awardees, who reaped honors for Cebu, there is, alas, only one survivor [as of 1983]: Dr. Ines Villa González, in her late eighties, still writing her fourth and final, novel in Spanish.

Even outside the Philippines, great Cebuano writers have made their mark. Their names are perpetually enshrined in books and dictionaries in various European libraries. To cite an example: our family *Diccionario de la Lengua Española* de la decimo-octava edición, published by the Real Academia Española, in Madrid, in 1956, lists the following Filipino members of the Academia Filipina: Sr. D. Guillermo Gómez, director, Sr. D. Jaime C. de Veyra, secretario, Sr. D, José Lauchengco, vice-secretario, Sr. D. Antonio M. Abad, censor, Sr. D. Emeterio Barcelón, bibliotecario, Sres. Ramón V. Torres, D. Claro M. Recto, D. Maríano Jesus Cuenco, D. Pedro Sabido, D. Pascual B. Azanza, D. Manuel C. Briones, D. Manuel B. Bernabé, D. Francisco Liongson, Arsenio N. Luz, D. Jorge Bocobo, D. Lorenzo Perez-Tuells and D. Enrique Fernandez Lumba.

I note with great pride that of the seventeen Filipinos, pillars of the prestigious Real Academia Española of Spain, there are three Cebuanos: Prof. Antonio M. Abad, Senator Manuel B. Briones, and Senator Maríano Jesus Cuenco.

The brilliance of those eminent Cebuano men of letters today serves as an inspiration for young writers who might be able to recapture for us those days of greatness and, perhaps, bring back in this decade of the Eighties a renaissance of the Cebuano, and Filipino, a golden era for literature and journalism (in Spanish).

※

IN 1915, DEAN C. Worcester arrived in Cebu City purportedly to lead a coconut oil refining company in Mactan. However, some older Filipinos were skeptical of his motives and claimed that he was one of many American spies earlier sent to the Philippines to assess the Spanish-Filipino military defense capabilities in preparation for the U.S. war with Spain. The aim was to acquire territories including the Philippines, Cuba, Puerto Rico, and Guam. Worcester had visited the Philippines in 1889 as a student to study Philippine birds.

In 1899, President McKinley of the United States formed the Schurman Commission to examine the situation in the Philippines and provide advice on how the country should proceed with its newly acquired territory from Spain. Worcester was among the commission's members. In 1908, the nationalist newspaper *El Renacimiento* published an editorial titled "Birds of Prey," accusing American officials of corruption and government crimes against the people. Worcester brought a lawsuit against the newspaper's writers for libel before an American judge. The judge shut down the newspaper, confiscated its assets and printing machines, jailed its publisher and writers, imposed martial law fines, and banned the use of Spanish and display of the Filipino flag. Besides the unjust "Aves de rapiña" ruling, the United States also committed severe police and military atrocities, including torture, on-the-spot hangings, and executions against Filipinos. Additionally, the flag and brigandage law prohibited private meetings and assemblies of all Filipinos.

Despite the cruel and tyrannical acts committed by American officials, including Worcester, the public villain in the eyes of present-day Filipinos is not Worcester or any other American government official. Instead, it is Padre Dámaso, a fictional character created by Rizal. In the wake of the "Aves de rapiña" scandal, Worcester turned to short film production as a hobby, depicting Filipinos as savages and dog eaters, unfit for self-government and political independence. He traveled to American newspapers, clubs, and universities, where he would lecture and screen his films for a curious American audience. For more information on

Worcester's anti-Filipino campaign, interested parties should consult Nick Deocampo's book *Film: American Influences on Philippine Cinema*.

Worcester's aggressive efforts to oppose Filipino independence were widely recognized among the Cebuano Spanish-speaking intelligentsia. This recognition prompted citizens to organize a protest against him at Cine Oriente. His trip to Cebu raised collective concern about his actions, which were deemed detrimental to the Filipino struggle for freedom. The written protest against him, in the Cebuano version, declares Worcester as the greatest enemy of Filipinos: "ang Americanhon nga labing contra sa mga Filipinhon..."

In line with Worcester's campaign to portray Filipinos as savages, Don Miguel Cuenco, a six-term congressman from Cebu, revealed that it was Worcester who selected Lapu-Lapu as a "savage hero" for Filipinos. He considered Filipinos to be savages, particularly the Cebuanos whose Spanish and Visayan press attacked him. Don Miguel, an erudite historian, guided us in reading from the book *Crónicas Visayas* (UST Press, 1917) by Esteban Lanza from Iloilo, which describes a committee resolution drawn in Cebu to erect the first monument.

In Opon, Mactan, Lapu-Lapu is often referred to as a "native hero who killed the invader Magellan." However, Catholic Bishop Juan Perfecto de Gorordo y Garcés, a Cebuano who was of Parián Chinese and Spanish mestizo descent, opposed this portrayal of Magellan as a "Spanish invader" because he was actually a Portuguese mariner-explorer-merchant with a financial contract with the Spanish King. The true invaders of the country were the Americans, who occupied Manila with their powerful battleships. Magellan, on the other hand, gave Cebuanos their Santo Niño, Mama Mary, and their first cross as symbols of peace and brotherhood, which led to their acceptance of Jesus Christ as their savior and the King of Spain as their ruler, making them Spaniards and Spanish citizens for over three centuries.

The knowledgeable Cebuanos understood that there was never a "battle" of Mactan, as it was actually an "ambush" of Magellan and his few men by "two hundred cowardly savages," as stated by Binondo chino cristiano poet Carlos Calao in 1614. Historian Danilo Gerona's recent research indicates that Lapu-Lapu could not have fought Magellan "because he was already a seventy-year-old man" in 1521. This invalidates the narrative inspired by the propaganda-laced Hispanophobia about old man Lapu-Lapu being an indigenous "hero against the invading Spaniards" meaningless.

CHAPTER XXVI
EXTRAORDINARY CITIZENS DRIVE ILOILO FORWARD

The invaluable photographs of Félix Laureano, considered as the first Filipino professional photographer, and their corresponding printed materials could have been lost to the ravages of time. But thanks to the efforts of an Ylongo corporate executive hailing from Tanza, Palapala and old Arévalo, these photos have been rescued and preserved. Through these photographs, the splendor and significance of Iloilo's history, art, culture, and politics are brought to life. It's worth noting that the old municipality of Arévalo boasts of a massive church and a monument to Queen Isabel II of Spain.

FRANCISCO "FRANK" VILLANUEVA Y GONZALO, who saved these invaluable treasures from being forgotten, spent his childhood in the vicinity of the public market of Iloilo, where he honed his photography skills by capturing images of the streets of León and Rizal. Villanueva attended the University of the Philippines and worked as a teacher before securing an executive position in an American company based in Manila. Eventually, he migrated to Canada, pursued higher education, learned French, and became a successful broadcaster. After retiring, he funded his own historical research, which led him to discover the significance of Laureano, a pioneering Filipino photographer with connections to Iloilo and Antique. With his proficiency in French, Villanueva was able to gain a better understanding of Spanish, allowing him to delve into the city's distant past.

In 2010, while on a visit to Valladolid, Spain, Villanueva was introduced to the works of Laureano. This encounter sparked a three-year personal project on Laureano, which culminated in an exhibit titled "Bugasong to Barcelona: Life & Works of Félix Laureano. The First Filipino Photographer." The exhibit, which showcased Laureano's photographs, was held under the auspices of the National Museum of the Philippines. Villanueva's tireless efforts did not go unnoticed, as the College of Arts and Sciences and the Center for West Visayan Studies of the University of the Philippines have supported his project since 2012. The success of the exhibit has inspired Frank to mount a Laureano photo exhibition in Iloilo and Manila in 2022.

NICK DEOCAMPO is another contemporary and heroic Ylongo soul. This film researcher from Negros Occidental has challenged the false history

Nick Deocampo

Frank Villanueva is photographed with Dr. Jurgenne Primavera, a National Museum of the Philippines trustee, and Jorell Legazpi, the deputy director-general for Museums, during the inauguration of the "Bugasong to Barcelona: Life and Works of Félix Laureano, First Filipino Photographer" photo exhibit on August 19, 2022, at the Western Visayas Regional Museum in Iloilo City.

and cultural narratives imposed on the current educational system. His revolutionary studies and research in film have exposed the misleading neocolonial paradigm. He has uncovered the forgotten Spanish chapter in the history of Filipino movies, disproving the narrative propagated by American colonialism that the Philippine film industry began and ended with American influence. Deocampo has proven that the film industry is another legacy of Spain that enriches Filipino civilization. By popularizing this fact, he shattered the old self-serving narrative on film, opened the eyes of many misled Filipinos, and highlighted their rich Spanish heritage. He has contributed significantly to the preservation and promotion of Philippine culture and history.

Deocampo's book, *Cine: Spanish Influences on Early Cinema in the Philippines*, which is the first volume of a five-book series on local film history, provides new data on the forgotten Spanish chapter of Filipino movies. While we appreciate Deocampo's efforts in uncovering this aspect of Philippine cinema history, we have reservations about how this study will ultimately impact the definition and establishment of "indigenous" and Filipino cinema. We believe that the Filipino identity has already been infused with Spanish influences, and that it cannot be resurrected with the invented Abakada culture that is erroneously passed off as "indigenous."

JOSÉ MARI CHAN Y LIM is another Ylongo who should not be overlooked. While he is well-known for the cheerful Christmas songs he composed and still performs, his personal significance to many of our Iloilo memories goes beyond that. There is a story associated with both of his parents that could have altered the life and destiny of this writer.

José Mari's parents, Papa Antonio Chan and Florence Chan, were so fond of this writer that they wanted to secure his future by arranging a marriage with a wealthy heiress named Mickey or Michaela Noronha from Macao, who could speak both Cantonese and Portuguese. They believed that our Spanish vernacular would make us a good fit for the Portuguese-speaking community in Macao, where they could run a luxury casino theatre restaurant. However, our adopted mother, Doña Rosa Jiménez Gayoso de Rivera, had other plans for us and sent us to Manila to work for Soriano and Company, leaving no room for the proposed marriage.

José Mari Chan

The swift decision made it possible to escape the envisioned wedding and honeymoon in faraway Venezuela that was planned by Florence Chan. If the proposal had gone through, we would have found ourselves living in Macao as a Chinese or Portuguese individual, disconnected from the culture and economic struggles that many Filipinos face today. However, this proposal is now just a sweet memory and an anecdote of a fantastic time.

NELIA JARUDA JOCSON used to be our partner and assistant in our younger years. As a young woman from Iloilo with roots in Parián de Molo, she collaborated with us to teach Spanish and Latin dances to our students, who greatly valued the physical and mental benefits of the classes. We even appeared in local publications, and Nelly's daughter and her niece became good Spanish dancers.

Mayen Gómez Lizares

Meanwhile, TERESA VILLANUEVA DE VARGAS, daughter of a prominent hacienda and real estate magnate, opened a flamenco school in her Iloilo and Manila mansions. She taught flamenco to American students from the military bases, including Bob and Honora Forescutt. The author's daughter, MAYEN GÓMEZ LIZARES, also became an excellent Spanish dancer, and together with her husband, she opened a dance school in Bacolod City, known as the sugar capital of the Philippines since the Spanish era. The school was well-attended.

In the 1960s, the former students of Colegio de San José in Jaro, led by Doña MARUJA PACHECO DE YULO, the widow of former provincial Governor Don José Yulo, organized Spanish dance performances and plays. During two or three reunions, the alumnae dressed in vibrant Spanish attire and danced Andalusian dances to the popular Orquesta Salinas. The Sisters of Charity who managed the school were thrilled and proud of their institution and distinguished alumnae, who looked and sounded so different from their now silent and gloomy English-trained students. Lola Marú Yulo and her peers were possibly the last group of graduates to receive an education in Spanish. Subsequent generations unwittingly carried the burden of cultural decline, ignorance, poverty, and social violence caused by the lack of emphasis on Filipino culture in the new curriculum introduced over the previous fifty years.

ANNIE DIVINAGRACIA-SARTORIO, a few years ago, orchestrated a Spanish flamenco performance at the newly refurbished Casa Gobierno, which shone a spotlight on Iloilo's cultural scene. This widely attended event was made possible through the assistance of then-Governor Arthur Defensor Jr. and then-acting Iloilo Mayor José Espinosa III. Annie, a dance teacher, paid tribute to the Spanish cultural heritage of Iloilo through her flamenco recital called "Abre Salón." The event was named after Doña María Felipe Villanueva's veladas held in her former Molo mansion and Don Vicente López' grandes fiestas españolas in his iconic Nelly Garden Mansion, which featured memorable flamenco performances by Chloe Cruz Periquet, María Vicenta Gamboa "Baby" Bonin, Mini del Rosario Lizares, and Rubén Nieto.

As of now, Divinagracia-Sartorio has been appointed as a National Commission for Culture and the Arts (NCCA) executive officer. She is married to Joerem Sartorio, a public servant in Iloilo City who values the historical significance of Iloilo's title as "la muy leal y noble ciudad" of Royal origin. Upon learning that Ylongos never rebelled against Spain, Joerem was moved by this fact.

Annie Divinagracia-Sartorio

Joe Marie Agriam

Filmmaker HENRY C. TEJERO has recently finished an extensive documentary on Jaro, which may offer a fresh perspective on Iloilo compared to other video productions. While other documentaries have been made on Iloilo, Tejero's work could potentially shed light on unique aspects of the city's new image. Despite focusing on Jaro exclusively, Tejero's documentary features the present-day voices of Iloilo's cultural icons and historians, including Demetrio Sonza and Nereo Cajilig Luján.

Tejero, a filmmaker from Tigbauan, has introduced us to the González Claravall family of Iloilo, who we have discovered to be our distant relatives. Among them is RICHIE GONZÁLEZ Y TAMONAN, who is married to ballet mistress Nila Claravall and is also Tejero's nephew. Richie was raised in the Gómez-Windham/Vital-García-González ancestral houses located at the corner of Zamora and Rosario streets near the old Plaza Libertad, which reminded us of the bygone glory of old Iloilo, characterized by its Vigan-like charm, Lenten processions, fiestas, and even bullfights at Durán-Tap-oc. Unfortunately, these ancestral houses are no longer standing.

LUTH SALUDES DE CAMIÑA AVANCEÑA appears to be preserving the traditions of Hispanic culture in Villa de Arévalo. Visiting her balay nga bató would be an intriguing experience, where one could witness the timeless Chino Cristiano-Español-Ylongo charm firsthand and relish a traditional Hispanic meal.

It's great to hear that JOE MARIE AGRIAM is promoting Iloilo's glamour and wellness through his lifestyle magazine *Cream*. It's important to highlight the beauty and grace of the Iloilo woman and showcase the city's brilliant social set. It's through such efforts that Iloilo can continue to shine as a modern metropolis with a rich cultural heritage.

Due to space constraints, we cannot include all the noteworthy Ylongos in this piece, but we plan to honor them in a forthcoming book. Meanwhile, we want to acknowledge the admirable efforts of Atty. JOSÉ MARI TIROL, the young law dean at our alma mater, University of San Agustín, who advocates for the reintroduction of Spanish in our

José Mari Tirol

education system. He believes that Spanish can be integrated into primary and intermediate levels, as it complements our major native languages and English. Later on, it can be an elective in high school and college. At present, the absence of Spanish in our schools is a glaring aberration.

It is imperative for the NCCA to establish a division for Spanish culture and heritage, as the evidence of our Spanish inheritance is undeniable. President Ferdinand Romuáldez Marcos Jr. recently emphasized the importance of emulating national hero José Rizal, including his proficiency in the Spanish language. This sentiment is reflected in Presidential Decree No. 155 issued by his late father, which designates Spanish as an official language for specific purposes and recognizes it as a valuable heritage shared with Hispanic countries, whose combined population exceeds half a billion.

In addition, a prophecy dating back to 1840 underscores the responsibility of Filipino leaders to preserve and promote the use of the Spanish language among our people. Those who have neglected this responsibility, such as a former President who removed Spanish from the curriculum in 1987, have suffered political repercussions, as evidenced in the 2022 elections, when the Marcos presidential victory resulted in their near-total obliteration from political power, indicating that the Hispanic heritage of the Filipino population is a valuable inheritance that requires protection against unfair treatment, while initiatives to promote and assist the Hispanic community should be encouraged. ¡Adelante!

EPILOGUE

An Ylongo Poet in a Language Maelstrom

By Pierce Centina

Guillermo Gómez Rivera, a highly regarded writer, is intimately acquainted with the complex terrain of emotions and is known to pay homage to life's phases through his poetic works: birth, joy and suffering, and death. Nevertheless, Gómez Rivera sets himself apart from other poets who are content to simply express their sentiments. Instead, he employs poetry as a conduit to advance a noble cause, no matter how impractical it may seem. This cause, which he ardently champions, is the retention of Spanish as a subject taught in Philippine schools. Regrettably, this lifelong advocacy suffered a blow when the Philippine Constitution of 1987 abolished the teaching of Spanish and stripped it of its official language status. This shortsightedness robbed Filipinos of a vital key that could unlock their national identity.

The new constitution, drafted in the elation that ensued after the so-called People Power Revolution of 1986, failed to recognize the swelling wave of globalization. Today, Spanish-speaking Filipinos are highly sought after in call centers, which are the lifeblood of the current Philippine economy, as well as in Spanish-speaking nations.

Gómez Rivera's unwavering advocacy has been validated by the enthusiastic inclination of young Filipinos to acquire proficiency in Spanish, as it enables them to earn twice the income of their English-speaking counterparts in the business process outsourcing industry. Notably, this phenomenon emerged thirty-five years after the ratification of the constitution, which was drafted by a commission appointed by Corazon C. Aquino during her tenure as head of the revolutionary government with dictatorial powers.

Gómez Rivera prefers to see himself as a modern-day Don Quixote, constantly tilting at windmills. However, unlike the fictional character, his endeavors are not fruitless in this quest. His Spanish-language works echo the writings of notable Filipinos like Claro M. Recto and Epifanio de los Santos in their efforts to preserve the Spanish language as a fundamental component of the national identity. While his promotion of Spanish has drawn some criticism, it has garnered more praise. Without question, he is the most distinguished Filipino writer in

Spanish today, recognized not only in the Philippines but also in Spain and other Spanish-speaking countries around the globe.

In 1975, Gómez Rivera was awarded the prestigious Premio Zobel de Hispanidad for his play, *El caserón,* and his advocacy for the Spanish language. As a correspondent of La Real Academia Española de la Lengua, he is listed in the academy's official Spanish dictionary published annually.

Gómez Rivera, a master of languages, speaks and writes with ease in Spanish, English, Tagalog, and a few others. Yet, it is his fluency in Ylongo, his native tongue, that has led him to create an impressive body of poetic works. Through his verses, he has immortalized Ylongo poetry and provided a glimpse into what it means to be Visayan and Filipino.

In one of his poems, Gómez Rivera bemoans the exclusion of Ylongo in Western Visayan schools, replaced instead by Tagalog-based Filipino, imposed unilaterally by the education department. He poses a rhetorical question, "And are they not bent in imposing their language in our very own schools, province, and race over our native tongue?"

In another poem, he longs for Iloilo City, where he spent his early years. He describes it as a princess, voluptuously reclining upon the bosom of the Visayas. Even though he is now far away, he sees the city as a magical mirror reflecting his roots, his language, and the birthplace of his soul.

In 1977, at a gathering of Western Visayans in Manila, Amado Yuson, a celebrated Pampango poet, honored Gómez Rivera with the title of "Prince of Ylongo Poetry." Delfín Gumbán, the "King of Ylongo Poetry," who had taught Gómez Rivera both Visayan and Spanish, also expressed his pride in his former student. He declared that Gómez Rivera was the only one deserving of such recognition and that his teacher, Don Flavio Zaragoza Cano, would have been proud of him if he were still alive.

This recognition of Gómez Rivera's literary works was significant because it marked the first time that the Ylongo language had been given national recognition by one of its most prominent advocates. The Ylongo communities in Visayas and Mindanao celebrated this achievement, as his works had brought together the Ylongo and Cebuano languages.

Gómez Rivera's steadfast defense of the Spanish language has garnered him widespread recognition and admiration. His unwavering commitment to preserving and promoting this beloved language earned him the esteemed Premio Zobel, an honor that delighted the Spanish and Latin American diplomatic communities, as well as members of the prestigious Academia Filipina de la Lengua Española.

However, for those who possess an unbridled passion for the Visayan language and literature, Gómez Rivera is revered for his ardent efforts to elevate both Ylongo and Cebuano, in the face of the compulsory imposition of purist Tagalog disguised as "Pilipino" in the educational system mandated by the Department of Education. Such a courageous stand has earned him a special place in the hearts of Visayan language aficionados, who view him as a champion of linguistic diversity and cultural identity.

Amid a language policy that has long overlooked the significance of all native languages and their connection to the country's Hispanic roots, there are those who refuse to be silenced. Gómez Rivera is among the valiant few who have taken up their pens to champion linguistic equity. His unwavering commitment to educating the youth of his country has led him to write and share his thoughts through social media, illuminating the vital role of the Spanish language and other native tongues in shaping the Filipino identity.

Though he knows that the path ahead will be difficult, Gómez Rivera's resolute spirit refuses to give up. His latest work, for which this epilogue was written, serves as evidence of his steadfast conviction that the struggle for a truly inclusive and representative national language remains a vital and ongoing battle. He recognizes that the fight must continue, fueled by the unwavering belief that the rich diversity of the Filipino people deserves to be fully recognized and celebrated. And so, as he embarks on this new literary endeavor, Gómez Rivera stands as a beacon of hope for those who share his vision of a nation that embraces and uplifts all its people.

Photographic Credits

The book's publishers have taken every possible step to identify the copyright owners of the photographs included in it. In case there are any copyright holders that have not been acknowledged, the publishers kindly request them to come forward so that they can be recognized in subsequent editions.

1. José Rizal, page 1; Andrés Bonifacio, page 46. Adobe Express
2. Plaza Libertad, 3. *imtnews.net*
3. Iloilo Economic History Museum, 4. *puertoparrot.com*
4. Calle Real, 5. *dreamcatcherrye.blogspot.com*
5. Molo principalía home, 11; Arévalo tower, 127. John Tewell through Flicker
6. Yusay-Consing mansion, 11, *adobe.com;* Molo Catholic church, *expedia.com*
7. Renato Constantino, 12. *nameless.org.ph*
8. Plaza Alfonso XII, 3 (inset); Iloilo Customs House, 9, by Bernárdo Arelláno III; Nick Joaquín, 12; Rizal Shrine, 83, by patrickroque01; map, 98; Arévalo church convent, 102, by Iloilo Wanderer; Fort San Pedro, 130, by Bsrap; John Bowring, 128; Wesley Merritt, 147; U.S. Forces at Fort Antonio Abad, 148; Felipe Agoncillo, Pedro Paterno, 149; Jorge Manrique, 172. *wikipedia.org*
9. General Martín Teófilo Delgado, 18. AngatBrujaDeputa through Twitter
10. Rudymar "Dinggol" Divinagracia Araneta, 33. Facebook
11. Filipino and Spanish soldiers, 56. *mentideroliterario.es*
12. Father Maríano Gil, OSA, 79. *guttenberg.org*
13. León Kilát, 78. *negrosnowdaily.com*; monument, by eazytraveler through Flicker
14. Philippine call center, 69. *lajornadafilipina.com*
15. English only poster, 77. *collectanealinguistica.wordpress.com*
16. Poster, Inglisero, 79. Tim Pacis at *youtube.com/watch?v=tK_K_w31ulo*
17. Dean C. Worcester with a Negrito man, 100. *fisherpub.sjf.edu*
18. Hacienda de Calamba, 87. *haciendadecalamba.blogspot.com*
19. Emilio Villanueva, 6; Felipe Gómez-Windham, 7; Guillermo Gómez-Windham, 8; Gómez-Windhan mansion, 10; Committee on National Language debate, 97; Francisco B. Albano Jr., 101; Ybiernas family, 133; Delfín Gumbán, 170. Gómez-Rivera Photo Archives
20. Lope K. Santos, 107. *upslis.info*
21. Balangay, 118. *philippinesmyphilippines.wordpress.com*
22. Datus, 121. Antique Provincial Tourism and Cultural Affairs Office through the Philippine News Agency (PNA)
23. Municipio de Arévalo, 129. *search.library.wisc.edu*Rizal, 134. *bravofilipino.com*

24. President Ferdinand R. Marcos Jr., 140. *pbbm.com.ph*
25. Hotel de Oriente, 137. *lougopal.com*
26. Masonic symbols, 141. Tim Sloan/AFP/Getty Images through *history.com*
27. American soldiers in the seashore; Filipino combatant with captured cannon in a bamboo trench, 149. *philipinoamericanwar.com*
28. Economic cartoon, 157. *Philippine Cartoons: Caricature of the American Era*
29. Worcester, 159. University Of Michigan Photo Archives
30. Aves de rapiña editorial, 160; Fidel A. Reyes, 162. *heroicsteps.blogspot.com*
31. Guillermo Gómez Rivera, 166. *visayandailystar.com*
32. Zaragoza Cano Las Rimas poster, 167. *geronimocristobal.com*
33. Miller house ruins, 179. *mybeautifuliloilo.blogspot.com*
34. Magdalena Jalandoni, 170. Facebook. University of San Agustín Publications
35. Flavio Zaragoza Cano, 170. Facebook. Ilawod Courtyard & Country Club
36. Sugar mill, train on tracks, 180. *fsdpi.org*
37. Frank Villanueva, 201. *dailyguardian.com*
38. Pepe Alas, 61. Facebook page of Pepe Alas.

INDEX

A

abaca 45, 84, 110
Abád, Antonio 109
Abakada XIV, 30, 31, 34, 35, 41, 44, 47, 99, 100, 101, 102, 106, 107, 108, 109, 114, 115, 152, 153, 156, 159, 161, 162, 186, 190, 192, 201
Abakada-Balarila XIV, 31, 106, 107, 108, 162
Abecedario XIV, 100, 101, 103, 107, 114, 123
Abella, Domingo 16
abolished the teaching of Spanish 12, 207
Abu Sayyaf 58, 60
Acapulco 45, 126
Aclan 119
acta de capitulación 72
Aetas 118
Afghanistan 108
agenda 30, 35, 55, 64, 84, 102, 143, 187
Age of Exploration 41
aggression 7, 35
Aglipay, Gregorio 142
Agoncillo, Felipe 147, 149, 210
Agoncillo, Marcela 31
Agoncillo, Teodoro A. 30, 34, 64, 107
agricultores 45
agsadores 45
Aguinaldo XIV, 7, 8, 18, 25, 31, 32, 46, 47, 50, 51, 52, 53, 54, 65, 67, 71, 72, 77, 78, 79, 86, 142, 146, 147, 148, 153, 157, 158, 159, 160, 178, 190, 191, 192
Aguinaldo, Emilio XIV, 53, 54, 72, 148
Ajuy 128
Alas, Pepe 55, 56, 57, 58
Alas y Soriano, José Mario Alas. See also Alas, Pepe. 55
Albano, Francisco B. Jr. 101
Alberto family 135
Alcantara Monteclaro, Pedro 119
Al Capone 66
Aldaba-Lim, Estefanía 58, 60
Almario, Virgilio 101
almuerzo 4
Alunan de Lizares, Enrica 132
America II, VIII, 18, 133, 142, 146, 159, 172, 179
American 3, 6, 7, 8, 9, 17, 18, 19, 20, 24, 25, 26, 27, 30, 32, 34, 35, 38, 39, 40, 41, 46, 47, 50, 51, 52, 53, 54, 55, 56, 57, 64, 65, 66, 70, 73, 76, 77, 79, 80, 84, 86, 90, 91, 98, 99, 102, 109, 114, 115, 132, 133, 134, 137, 141, 142, 143, 146, 147, 148, 149, 152, 153, 156, 157, 158, 159, 160, 162, 170, 177, 178, 179, 181, 186, 196, 200, 201, 202, 208, 211
American colonial government 9, 160, 196
American invaders 6, 18, 24, 26, 27, 47, 51, 56, 57, 65, 79, 86, 146, 178
Americanized 30, 35, 44, 64, 133, 136, 148

American occupation 6, 18, 156
Americans XIV, 8, 9, 10, 12, 18, 20, 26, 27, 30, 38, 39, 40, 41, 46, 47, 50, 51, 53, 54, 56, 57, 64, 65, 71, 79, 90, 97, 98, 99, 133, 143, 146, 147, 148, 152, 157, 158, 159, 179, 190, 197
Americas 45
Andalusian dances 203
Anglican 6
Ang Maragtas sang Panay 16
Aninipay 118, 119, 166, 167, 168
anito 27
Antique 18, 119, 121, 167, 200, 210
aparcero 24
Aquino-Cojuangco political dynasty 140
Aquino, Corazon C. 81, 141, 207
Aquino-Marcos feud 141
Aquino, President Corazon C. 81
Aquino, Salustiano 135
Aquino, Senator Benigno S. 192
Arabesque-Andalusian style 188
Araneta, Gregorio S. 40
archipelago 6, 54, 111, 147, 156, 158, 161, 166, 167
Arévalo VIII, 126, 127, 129, 185, 200, 204, 210
arroceros 45
artist John Alaban 121
Asia 45, 52, 96, 110, 128, 141, 146, 156
Asian 132, 133
Asians 40, 41
asuang 16, 24, 26, 177
atrocities 9, 51, 196
Augustinian 34, 45, 119, 126
Austronesian 121, 123
Aves de rapiña 64, 84, 98, 100, 156, 160, 162, 211
A Visit to the Philippines 128
Azanza, Congressman Pascual B. 80, 152

B

Bacalso, Natalio 107, 191
Bacolod City, 202
Balagtas 100, 102, 107, 114
Balagtas, Francisco 100, 107
balangays 118
Balangiga massacre 64, 79, 80
Balarila XIV, 31, 100, 106, 107, 108, 162, 190
Balasan 128
Balayan 120
balay nga bato XIV, 26
balay nga bato kag tapi XIV
Balensuyela 120
Baler 47
balikbayans 90
Balintawak 84
Banco Español-Filipino de Isabel II de las Islas Filipinas 4

Banco Islas 4, 5
Bangcaya 119
Bangsamoro Autonomous Region 110
Banug 18
barangay 96, 118, 119
Barcelona 137, 200, 201
Barcelón y Barceló Soriano, Emeterio 84, 85
barrio 16, 17, 18, 24, 119, 177, 178
Barrio Jaguimit 178, 180
Barter of Panay 32, 122
Basa, José María 134
Batallón de Voluntarios XIV, 8, 32
Batallones de Cebuanos Leales XIV, 32
Batangas 65, 72, 120, 121
Batangueña 5
Batangueños 65, 120
Batista, Fulgencio 7
battalion 18, 65
Battle of Mactan 33
Baybayin 123
Behind the Lodge Door 56, 77, 142
benevolent assimilation 38, 143
Bicol 3, 77
Bicolano 45
Bicolanos 32, 61, 76, 120, 123, 153
Biden, President Joe 146
Biñán 135
Binisaya XIII
Binondo 78, 135, 136, 148, 186, 197
Binondo chino cristiano poet Carlos Calao 197
"Birds of Prey" 161
black arts 27
Blacks 41
Blaire, Emma Helen 64
Bohol 65, 66, 110, 111, 190
Bonifacio 31, 32, 47, 52, 56, 58, 59, 60, 61, 67, 71, 78, 79, 84, 176, 184, 190, 191, 210
Bonifacio Andrés 31, 52, 58, 59, 60, 67, 71, 78, 84, 191, 210
Bonifacio, Procopio 67, 71, 190
Bonin, María Vicenta Gamboa "Baby" 203
Bornean 24, 118, 119, 121, 122, 123, 166, 167
Bornean datus 24, 118, 119, 121, 122, 166, 167
Borneo 32, 118, 119, 120, 121, 166
botica 2
boticario 2, 4
Bowring, Sir John 128
Boxer Codex 35, 45
Briones, Manuel 109
British 5, 6, 53, 77, 128, 179
British consul 6
Bugasong to Barcelona: Life & Works of Félix Laureano. First Filipino Photographer. 200
Bulacan 188
bureaucrats 30
Burgos, Padre José Apolonio 142
Burton Harrison, Governor-General Francis 56, 59, 98

C

Cabaliststs 27
Cadíz 39
Cagayan de Misamis 76
Cajilig Luján, Nereo 204
Calamba 6, 84, 85, 86, 87, 135, 136, 210
Calinog 16
Calle Bonifacio 176
Calle Colón 194
Calle Durán XIV
Calle Estraude 135
Calle Fernando 135
Calle Iznart 5, 184
Calle Ledesma 184
Calle Progreso 2
Calle Real 2, 4, 5, 127, 184, 210
Calle Santo Rosario XIII
Cantonese 202
capital punishment 137
Capiz 16, 18, 72, 78, 180
carabao 45, 123
Carcar 8, 78, 79, 188, 189, 190
Caribbean 190
Carles 128
carruaje 2, 136
Casa Gobierno 184, 203
Casa Gorordo 194
Casa Real 5, 127, 184
Casino Español XIV, 127, 132, 184, 185
Castilian 167, 170, 173, 192
Castro, Fidel 7, 61
catalog 16, 17
Catálogo Alfabético de Apellidos 16
catechism 38
Catholic 3, 4, 11, 38, 41, 44, 46, 50, 57, 58, 59, 60, 77, 84, 110, 123, 126, 127, 141, 152, 177, 186, 197, 210
Catholic Church 4, 57, 77, 84, 123, 177
Catholicism 6, 9, 38, 44, 61
Catholic nation 46, 141
Catholization 44
Cavite 9, 52, 53, 67, 71, 77, 96, 142, 190
Cavite Mutiny 142
Caviteño 52
Cebu IX, 8, 18, 31, 45, 46, 54, 76, 78, 79, 99, 107, 110, 111, 119, 122, 152, 159, 184, 185, 186, 187, 188, 189, 190, 191, 192, 193, 194, 195, 196, 197
Cebuano II, III, XI, XIII, 18, 32, 35, 53, 64, 66, 67, 70, 78, 79, 99, 109, 162, 186, 187, 188, 190, 191, 192, 194, 195, 196, 197, 208
Cebuanos XIV, 7, 8, 9, 32, 47, 55, 64, 67, 79, 80, 115, 160, 190, 194, 195, 197
Celso Ledesma Building XIV
Centina, Pierce II, 207
Centiramo Publishing II
Central Azucarera de Dumalág 24

Chan, Antonio 202
Chan, Florence 202
Chan y Lim, José Mari 201
Charleston American Lodge 56
Chavacano 96
China 77, 108, 141, 142, 146, 149
Chinatown 186
Chinese XIV, 40, 50, 73, 78, 96, 100, 114, 123, 126, 127, 128, 132, 146, 148, 179, 180, 185, 186, 187, 188, 190, 197, 202
chino cristiano 3, 40, 45, 47, 50, 76, 78, 79, 84, 100, 127, 128, 132, 185, 187, 189, 197
chino-cristiano culture 148
Chino Cristiano-Español-Ylongo charm 204
Chinóy (Tsinoy) 90
Christian 38, 41, 55, 57, 58, 59, 60, 110, 128, 186, 190
Cine: Spanish Influences on Early Cinema in the Philippines 201
citizenship 36, 38, 39, 46
Ciudad de Iloilo 2, 50
Ciudad Española 127, 185
Civil Rights Movement 41
Claravall, Nila 204
Clark Air Base 132
Claveria y Zaldúa, Governor-General Narciso 16
clergy 44, 142, 143
client state 47, 51
cochero 2
Código de Calanti-ao, 32
Código de Sumacuel 32
Cold War 141
colonialism 20, 27, 30, 31, 35, 40, 79, 91, 201
colonial rulers 26, 47
colonization XIV, XV, 10, 20, 38, 39, 47, 109, 110, 143
colonizers 32, 34, 51, 80, 86, 99, 106, 115, 121
Colón Street 187
Committee on National Language 97, 101, 210
Commonwealth era 106
communist 149, 186, 191, 192
Communist Party of the Philippines 192
composos 16, 168, 169
Concepción, Venancio 18, 50
Confederation of Madia-as, alternatively spelled as Madya-as and Madja-as 118, 122
conquistadores 41, 44, 46, 123, 126, 127, 167
Constantino, Renato 12, 210
constitution 12, 39, 96, 101, 102, 109, 190, 191
convents 38
coplas 169, 172
Córpuz, Onofre D. 55, 60
Corrales, Manuel 76
corrido-awit literature 123
corridos 16, 168
corridos antiguos 168
corridos modernos 168
corruption 20, 39, 44, 58, 60, 108, 140, 152, 154, 156, 160, 196
Coscuella mansion 10
Cotabato 122

country XIII, XIV, 3, 4, 7, 8, 10, 12, 13, 20, 25, 26, 30, 31, 38, 39, 44, 45, 46, 51, 52, 53, 54, 56, 57, 58, 60, 61, 70, 71, 72, 73, 90, 91, 92, 93, 96, 97, 101, 106, 107, 115, 128, 129, 134, 135, 141, 142, 143, 146, 148, 152, 153, 157, 161, 162, 172, 173, 176, 179, 186, 188, 190, 191, 192, 193, 196, 197, 209
Covid-19 39, 108, 141, 160
Creole 46, 96, 142, 184, 185
criollos 185
Cristóbal, Valentín 169
Crónicas Visayas 20, 197
Cruz Periquet, Chloe 203
Cry of Pugad Lawin 78
Cry of Santa Bárbara 25
Cuba 3, 7, 17, 55, 70, 77, 137, 157, 196
Cuenco, Congressman Miguel 80
cuentos 16
cultural colonialism 35
cultural heritage V, XIII, 12, 13, 30, 31, 81, 92, 106, 107, 142, 190, 193, 203, 204
cultural identity XIV, 30, 209
curriculum 30, 32, 99, 102, 203, 205

D

Dagohoy, Francisco 65, 66
Dapitan 2, 4, 9, 58, 60, 70, 136, 137
Dator 17
datu 24, 118, 122
Datu Domalogdog 24
Datu Puti 24, 118, 119, 120, 121
datus 24, 118, 119, 120, 121, 122, 123, 166, 167
Davao 76
Dayot 17, 177
de-Christianize 142, 143
Dedication V, 34
Defensor, Governor Arthur Jr. XIII, 203
de-Hispanization 103
De la Rama, Don Félix 50
Delgado XIII, XIV, 17, 18, 25, 33, 47, 70, 71, 72, 73, 184, 210
Delgado, General Martín Teófilo XIII, XIV, 17, 18, 25, 33, 47, 70, 71, 210
Del Mar, Professor José María 109, 193, 195
De Ovando, Nicolás 41
De los Reyes, Ventura 39
De los Ríos, Governor-General Diego 65, 70,71, 72
De los Santos, Epifanio 207
Del Pilar, Marcelo H. 58, 60
Del Rosario Lizares, Mini 203
Deocampo, Nick 196, 200, 201
De Ovando, Nicolás 41
Department of Education 90, 102, 108, 152, 208
Despujol, Governor-General Eulogio 136, 137
De Veyra, Jaime C. 193, 195
De Villanueva, María Felipe 3, 134
Dewey, Admiral George 53, 70, 146
Día Español de Santiago 132
Díaz Laurel, Celia 77

Diego Jiménez Frades 184
Diez Datos de Borneo 32
diglossia 97
Dimaculañgan, María Nelia 5
Dingle 17, 18, 19, 24, 25, 26, 27, 176, 177
Diokno, General Ananías 25, 72
disciplinario 76
discrediting the legitimacy of the Republic of the Philippines 158
discrimination 41
Divinagracia, Rudymar "Dinggol" Araneta 31, 32
Divinagracia-Sartorio, Annie 203
Domalogdog 24
Dominican 6, 9, 47, 84, 85, 86, 126, 135, 136
Dominican Order 9, 47, 85,
Villanueva, Doña María Felipe 3, 134
Don Juan Tiñoso 16, 168
Donoso, Isaac 97
Don Quijote, XI
Drilon, Senator Franklin XIII
Gómez y de Arce, Doctor José María 5
Dueñas VII, 18, 19, 24, 25, 26, 177, 178, 180, 181
Duke of Wharton 77
Dumalág 24, 180
Dumalogdog 17
Dumangas 128
Dumangsil 120
Dutch attacks 126
Dutch East Indies 126
Duterte, President Rodrigo 61

E

Eagle Theatre 185
education XIII, 10, 27, 30, 35, 64, 76, 79, 80, 86, 90, 91, 92, 93, 99, 102, 108, 115, 136, 152, 168, 170, 176, 186, 188, 200, 203, 205, 208
education system 30, 91, 92, 205
El Adalid 20, 132
El caserón 208
El Heraldo 20, 132
El Nuevo Día 192, 193
El Polvorín 71
El Porvenir de Visayas 20, 50, 184
El Renacimiento 98, 160, 195, 196
embargo 7
empadronamiento 16, 24
encomienda 186, 190
encomienda y pueblo 186
Encyclopedia of the Peoples of Asia and Oceania 156
England 77
English V, XIV, 6, 27, 56, 77, 79, 80, 81, 90, 91, 92, 93, 97, 99, 102, 103, 109, 115, 123, 132, 133, 152, 160, 169, 176, 178, 187, 191, 192, 194, 195, 203, 205, 207, 208, 210
Equatorial Guinea 148
España XI
española 5, 127
Espinosa, Mayor José XIII, 203
Estado Federal de Visayas 32, 35, 64, 115

ethnic groups 25, 31, 32, 184
Europe 40, 45, 84, 85, 194
European 45, 46, 84, 141, 142, 143, 146, 156, 190, 195
evangelization 44
exclusion 31, 34, 38, 208
exile 2, 4, 7, 8, 53, 58, 60, 136
expeditionary force 25

F

false narrative 32, 47, 76
Federalist Party 40
Felipe II XI
Fernán, Marcelo 191
fiestas 19, 128, 177, 203, 204
Filipina 8, 18, 58, 60, 71, 136, 178, 195, 208
Filipinas XI, 4, 7, 27, 32, 35, 41, 45, 46, 52, 53, 58, 60, 70, 72, 77, 84, 86, 99, 101, 102, 103, 114, 152, 160, 178, 190, 195
Filipino XIV, 3, 4, 7, 8, 10, 16, 20, 26, 34, 35, 38, 41, 44, 45, 46, 51, 52, 53, 55, 56, 57, 59, 61, 64, 67, 72, 73, 77, 78, 79, 80, 81, 86, 90, 92, 97, 98, 99, 100, 101, 102, 106, 108, 109, 114, 115, 122, 123, 133, 134, 137, 141, 142, 143, 147, 149, 152, 153, 156, 158, 159, 160, 162, 163, 166, 170, 172, 178, 179, 186, 187, 189, 190, 191, 192, 195, 196, 200, 201, 203, 205, 207, 208, 209, 210, 211
Filipino cinema 201
Filipino-Hispano Ilustrado order 186
Filipino people 8, 10, 26, 79, 86, 99, 109, 115, 141, 143, 152, 187, 190, 209
Filipinos XIV, 8, 10, 12, 13, 27, 30, 31, 35, 38, 39, 40, 44, 46, 51, 52, 54, 56, 58, 60, 61, 72, 76, 80, 81, 86, 87, 92, 98, 99, 100, 101, 109, 132, 133, 143, 147, 148, 149, 152, 153, 156, 157, 158, 159, 160, 162, 163, 166, 179, 187, 192, 195, 196, 197, 201, 202, 207
Film: American Influences on Philippine Cinema 196
First Globalization 148
Fisher, Paul A. 77, 142
flamenco XI, 177, 178, 194, 202, 203
Florante at Laura 100, 102, 107
Floyd, George 41
Ford-Garcia family 24
Ford-Garcia sugarcane mill 180
Ford, Thomas 179
forebears 31, 32, 120
foreign debt 38
foreign influence 38
foreign invaders 16
Fort San Pedro XIV, 5, 133, 210
Frades, Diego Jiménez 184
frailes 38, 45
France 142
Francisco y Tuáson, Domingo 77
Fray Camorra 84
Fray Salvi 84
Freemasonry 57, 59, 61, 77, 85, 142, 143
Freemasons 142

French 65, 200
friar 6, 34, 38, 44, 45, 47, 57, 58, 59, 60, 61, 77, 79, 84, 85, 86, 99, 123, 126, 130, 134, 135, 142, 143, 190
Fuerte de San Pedro 127
Fukien-Ua 3
Fundamental Principles of the Hiligaynon Language 101

G

Galleon Trade 45, 148
Gantuangco Briones, Concepción 187, 188, 192
Garcia, María 179
Gavira 17, 177
Gayoso 17
Gayoso, Victoriano 184
General 18, 53, 56, 59, 71, 72, 147
geopolitical gamesmanship 141
Germany 84, 142
Gerona, Danilo 66, 197
Gil, Father Mariano, OSA 77, 79, 210
Gliceria Marella 65, 72
gobernadorcillo 17, 132, 135
God 3, 38, 59, 72, 172
Go, Julian 40
Dimaculañgan 5
Gómez, Francisco "Paco" 176
Gómez Lizares, Mayen 202
Gómez Monfort, Francisco 5
Gómez Rivera, Guillrmo II, III, XI, 27, 166, 178, 207, 211
Gómez-Windham 4, 5, 10, 179, 204, 210
Gómez y Windham, Felipe 2, 7
González Claravall family 204
Gónzalez, Fred 176
González y Tamonan, Richie 204
Gonzalves, Theodore S. 147
Gorordo y Perfecto, Father Juan Bautista 18. See also Bishop Gorordo.
Government Service Insurance System (GSIS) XIII
Governor-General 56, 59, 72
grandfather 2, 4, 5, 6, 24, 65, 77, 176, 178, 179, 180
Gran Oriente Español 77
Gran Oriente Lodge 56
Guam 3, 17, 157, 196
guardias civiles 66
Guerrero, León Ma. 86
guerrilla revolt 8
Guillerán 16, 17, 24
Guimarás Island 17, 180
Guimbal 17, 111
Gumbán, Delfín 34, 109, 115, 119, 120, 170, 171, 208, 210
Gumbán, Eriberto 169
gunboats 18, 76
Gutierrez, Luis 176

H

hacendero 24, 45, 50, 79
hacienda 3, 6, 45, 84, 85, 86, 135, 136, 176, 180, 190, 202
Halad Kay San Roque 170
Hamilton Club 158
Hamtic 121
hendecasyllable 168, 170
Henry Scott, William 32
heritage V, XIII, XIV, XV, 12, 13, 30, 31, 34, 35, 44, 55, 81, 92, 93, 101, 106, 107, 142, 162, 179, 187, 188, 189, 190, 193, 201, 203, 204, 205
Hernández, Adriano 18, 72
hero 56, 59
Hiligaynon V, XIII, XIV, XV, 5, 16, 91, 96, 101, 102, 115, 119, 120, 166, 167, 170, 173, 180
Hiniray-a (or Kinaray-a) 166
Hispanic VIII, IX, 24, 32, 33, 34, 55, 100, 109, 114, 118, 120, 121, 123, 133, 148, 156, 161, 162, 166, 173, 186, 187, 188, 192, 194, 204, 205, 209
hispanista 9, 55, 99
Hispanophobia 41, 80, 93, 96, 114, 135, 159, 197
history XIII, XIV, XV, 8, 10, 12, 13, 24, 28, 30, 31, 32, 33, 34, 35, 39, 44, 47, 51, 52, 53, 55, 56, 57, 62, 64, 65, 67, 73, 76, 79, 80, 81, 84, 86, 87, 90, 91, 92, 93, 99, 106, 107, 110, 114, 118, 120, 121, 132, 137, 138, 140, 141, 142, 143, 146, 157, 159, 166, 167, 168, 185, 187, 188, 190, 192, 193, 194, 200, 201, 211
History of California 40
Hong Kong 6, 7, 8, 21, 51, 53, 86, 128, 136, 147, 157, 158
Hotel Oriente 136
Howe Bancroft, Hubert 40
Humanum Genus 57
hurubatons 16

I

"I can't breathe." 41
identity XIV, XV, 13, 21, 30, 32, 80, 81, 90, 99, 106, 109, 114, 115, 153, 162, 163, 186, 192, 201, 207, 209
Igorot 98, 100, 156, 161
Iligan 76
Ilocanos 32, 110, 123, 153, 166, 192
Ilocos 45
Iloilo VII, VIII, IX, XIII, XIV, 2, 3, 4, 5, 6, 7, 9, 10, 11, 16, 18, 20, 21, 24, 25, 26, 27, 30, 31, 45, 46, 47, 50, 64, 65, 70, 71, 72, 73, 76, 78, 91, 101, 110, 111, 114, 115, 119, 121, 126, 127, 128, 129, 132, 134, 135, 152, 176, 178, 179, 180, 181, 184, 185, 186, 190, 192, 197, 198, 200, 201, 202, 203, 204, 208, 210
Iloilo Economic History Museum 4, 210
Iloilo River Bridge and Esplanade XIV
Ilongo 166
Ilustrados 34, 55, 84, 156, 179
Imang 16
IMF 108, 187. See also International Monetary Fund
imperialists 40

inasuañgon 16
independence XIII, XIV, 8, 10, 30, 40, 54, 72, 73, 76,
    86, 87, 98, 141, 147, 148, 156, 157, 158, 172,
    196
independent II, III, VII, XI, XIII, 28, 142
indianeta 17
Indians 40, 41, 147, 157
indigenous 38, 41, 101, 162, 166, 167, 184, 190, 197,
    201
indio 40, 45, 90, 126, 128, 132, 179, 185
Indonesia 126
inglisera 90
inglisero 88, 90, 91, 93
insurrectos and revolucionarios 18
International Monetary Fund 90, 102, 141. See also IMF
Intramuros 111, 147, 148
invaders 6, 16, 18, 24, 25, 26, 27, 47, 51, 56, 57, 65, 73,
    79, 86, 118, 146, 178, 197
invasion 8, 17, 20, 25, 26, 52, 91, 98, 142, 143, 146,
    148, 187
Iloilo City 24
Iran 108
Islam 118, 122
Italian 128
Italy 142

J

Agriam, Joe Marie 204
Jalandoni, Magdalena 115, 170, 172, 211
Jalaud River 177
Japan 142
Japanese 20, 56, 132, 148, 169, 176, 187
Japanese-American War 20
Japanese Occupation 169
Jareños 50
Jaro 18, 50, 71, 72, 76, 127, 128, 132, 179, 184, 186,
    203, 204
Jaruda Jocson, Nelia 202
Jennifer López 97
Jepte-Sáenz Building 185
Jesuit 65, 126, 142, 193
Jesus Christ 197
Jewish 41
Jiménez Gayoso de Rivera, Rosa 176, 177, 202
Joan of Arc 64, 65
Joaquín, Nick 12, 52, 58, 60, 90, 191, 210
Joseph Beal Steere's expedition 157
Juan de la Cruz 157
Junto al Pasig 6

K

kaingeros 45
Kalaw, Teodoro M. 98, 109, 160
Kastila 41
Kastilaloy 90
Katilingban sang Madia-as 107
Katipunan VII, 7, 8, 9, 30, 31, 32, 44, 46, 47, 50, 52,
    55, 56, 57, 58, 59, 60, 67, 71, 76, 77, 78, 79,
    97, 99, 100, 135, 136, 137, 142, 143, 190
Katipuneros XIV, 8, 32, 46, 51, 56, 58, 59, 60, 61, 76,
    78, 190
Kinaray-a 16, 166, 167
King Maricudo 118
Komisyon sa Wikang Filipino 101, 102, 153, 162

L

Labao Dungon 27
La Cotta XIV, 5, 127, 133, 134
Laglag 17, 24
Laguda ruins XIV
Laguna 86, 87, 135, 190
la muy leal y noble ciudad 203
Lanao 76
language V, XIII, XIV, XV, 10, 12, 24, 31, 32, 38, 40,
    44, 46, 61, 80, 81, 91, 92, 93, 94, 96, 97,
    99, 100, 101, 102, 103, 106, 107, 108, 109,
    114, 115, 123, 133, 152, 153, 159, 160, 161, 162,
    163, 166, 167, 172, 173, 186, 191, 192, 193,
    194, 195, 205, 207, 208, 209
Lanza, Don Esteban 20, 197
Lanza, Rafael 20
Laoag 110
La Panayana XIII
La Paz 128, 184
Lapu-lapu 33, 34, 64, 66, 67, 197
La Real Academia Española de la Lengua 208
La Solidaridad 135
La Union 46, 110
Laureano, Félix 27, 200, 201
Laurel, Senator José P. 12
Laurel, Vice President Salvador H. 77
lawyer 2, 6, 55, 171, 193, 194, 195
Leales XIV, 8, 18, 32, 35, 53, 54, 64, 70, 78, 79, 148,
    190
Ledesma Hotel 184
Legarda, Benito 40
Lemery 128
León Kilát 8, 78, 79, 190, 210
Leyte 119, 152, 190, 193
Liberation, 168
Libertas 84
Lieutenant General Pantaleón Villegas y Soldi 8, 78, 79.
    See also León Kilát
Life in Old Parian 187, 188, 190, 192
lifestyle magazine *Cream* 204
Liga Filipina 58, 60, 136
linguistic and cultural illiteracy XIV
Lizares, Emiliano 185
Locsin-Araneta clan 6
Logia Taliba 58, 60
López, Vicente 203
Loney, Nicholas 5
Los Leales Cebuanos 8 See also Leales
Lubas sa Dagang Bisaya 107
Lumads 101, 122, 166
Luna, Dolores 46
Luna y Novicio, Joaquín 46

Luneta 77
Luther King, Martin Jr. 41
Luzon 25, 31, 53, 76, 79, 98, 120, 123, 190
Luzon 61, 120

M

Macao 202
Macapagal-Arroyo, Gloria 58, 60
Mactan 33, 66, 196, 197
Madia-as 27, 32, 107, 118, 119, 166
Madia-as Confederation 32, 119
Madre España XI
Madrid 2, 5, 135, 195
Magahum, Angel 169
Magalona, Senator Enrique 80, 152
Magbanua, Teresa 24, 64
Magdalo 52, 58, 60, 142
Magdiwang 52
Magellan, Ferdinand 33, 34, 66, 67, 159, 197
Maguindanao 122, 123, 166
Makati City XV
Malayo-Indo-Polynesian language 166
Malaysia 77, 126
Malolos 72
Malvar, General Miguel 54, 152
Mamalu 122
Mama Mary 197
Mancao, Luz 188
Mangyans 156, 157
Manifest Destiny 18
Manila VII, 2, 3, 6, 9, 18, 27, 32, 33, 35, 45, 47, 53, 54, 56, 67, 70, 71, 73, 76, 77, 84, 86, 96, 111, 115, 126, 132, 135, 136, 137, 146, 147, 148, 149, 158, 159, 167, 176, 180, 186, 190, 191, 193, 195, 197, 200, 202, 208
manipulation of Philippine history 10
Manrique, Jorge 172, 173, 210
Mapa, Don Victorino 50
Mapa y Lizares, Estrella 132
Mapa y Lizares, Plácido 132
Maragondon 71
Maragtas 16, 32, 33, 34, 35, 118, 119, 120, 121, 122, 123, 166
Maragtas sang Panay 16, 32
Marcos 61, 140, 141, 142, 190, 192, 205, 211
Marcos, President Ferdinand E. Sr. 40, 190, 192
Marcos y Romuáldez, Ferdinand Jr. 140
Marella, Gliceria 65
Maribojoc 111
Mari Tirol, Atty. José 204
Mark Twain 179, 194
Marquez-Lim, Manuel 185
Marquez-Lim, Pedro 127
Mason 3, 4, 6, 8, 57, 58, 60, 65, 78, 85, 100, 114, 135, 136, 142
Masonic VII, 7, 9, 47, 52, 55, 56, 57, 58, 59, 60, 77, 78, 84, 136, 142, 143, 147, 186, 190, 211
Masons 3, 7, 27, 31, 47, 50, 55, 56, 57, 71, 76, 77, 78, 80, 114, 134, 135, 142, 190

Maxilom y Molero, General Arcadio 18
May, Glenn Anthony 52
McKinley, President William 18, 40, 53, 58, 99, 156
Melliza, Raymundo 32
Mercado, Francisco 135
Merritt, General Wesley 147
mesticería 185
mestiza 3, 6, 85, 179
mestizaje 41
mestizo 18, 41, 71, 78, 84, 127, 168, 179, 189, 190, 197
mestizos 126, 128, 185
Mexican 123, 177, 186
Miag-ao 110
Miceli, Father Vincent 142
Miller 176
Miller, Anthony 177
Miller, Encarnación 20
Miller, General Marcus P. 18, 21, 25, 73
Miller, Henry 176
Mindanao 20, 25, 53, 70, 76, 101, 110, 115, 119, 122, 161, 172, 191, 192, 208
Mindanaoans 9, 25, 55, 76
Mindoro 156, 161
Misamis 76
missionaries 45, 78, 122, 126, 141, 166
mixed marriages 41
Mojares, Resil B. 187
Molo XIV, 2, 4, 11, 50, 71, 126, 128, 132, 134, 135, 202, 203, 210
Molo (St. Anne) Roman Catholic Parish Church 11
Monet, General Ricardo 70, 71, 72
Montero 17, 177
Montojo Pasarón, Rear Admiral Patricio 76
Moro 58, 60, 110, 111, 122, 126
Moroboro 177
Moro Islamic Liberation Front 58, 60
Moros 16, 122, 123
Moros y Cristianos 16
Moro Wars 110
mountain redoubt 18, 19
Mount Bulabog-Putian 18
Mount Buntis 52, 67, 190
Muelle Loney 5, 9, 127, 184
muscovado 24
Muslim 41, 110, 122
Muslims 110, 192
Mutual Defense Treaty 149
Muzones, Ramón L. 115
myth 33, 55, 121, 142

N

Namacpacan 46, 110
National Commission for Culture and the Arts (NCCA) 101, 203
National Museum of the Philippines 200, 201
NATO 146
Negros Occidental 45, 46, 107, 110, 132, 152, 181, 200
Nelly Garden Mansion 203
neocolonial 44, 84, 201

neocolonialism 64
neocolonization 35
neologisms 102, 103
Netflix 153, 106
New People's Army 78
New World 41
Nieto, Rubén 203
Noli Me Tangere 79

O

Obando 188
Ocampo, Martín 98
octosyllable 168
One China policy 146
Opon 197
oral traditions 16, 32, 33, 34, 168
Orient 71
Osmeña, Sergio 192
Oton 128
overseas territories 3, 7, 46, 190
Ozamiz, Julio 191

P

Paas, Anton 76
Pacheco de Yulo, Maruja 203
Pacific 126, 141, 146, 190
Pacto de Biacnabató 8, 53
Pact of Biacnabató 7, 51, 52, 53, 147
Padre Dámaso 79, 99, 160, 196
Pagsanjan 5
Paibúrong 119
Palawan 111
Palma, Rafael 193, 195
Pampanga 132
Pampangos 32, 76, 123, 153
Panay 16, 20, 24, 25, 27, 32, 33, 45, 118, 119, 120, 121, 122, 123, 126, 166, 167, 168
Panay Island 16, 20, 118, 166
pandilla-barcada 2
Pardo de Tavera, Trinidad 40, 114
Parián XII, 2, 11, 50, 79, 126, 127, 152, 180, 185, 186, 187, 188, 189, 190, 191, 192, 193, 197, 202
Parián de Cebu 79
Parián de Molo 2, 11, 50, 202
parianes 186, 190
Pasig River 106
Passi 65, 177, 186
patadiongs 24
Paterno, Pedro 147, 149
Patio Cementerio de Tanza 127
Pavía 119, 128
People Power Revolution 140, 207
People's Republic of China 146
Pepito, Gerardo 191
Philip II 38, 44
Philippine XIV, 5, 8, 9, 10, 12, 13, 16, 30, 31, 34, 40, 46, 50, 51, 52, 53, 55, 56, 59, 76, 79, 86, 90, 93, 97, 98, 99, 100, 101, 114, 137, 142, 143, 147, 148, 149, 152, 156, 157, 158, 159, 160, 178, 180, 181, 186, 188, 192, 196, 201, 207, 210, 211
Philippine-American War 8, 9, 30, 46, 50, 51, 52, 53, 79, 86, 147, 152, 159, 178, 181
Philippine Constitution 12
Philippine Daily Inquirer XIV
Philippine folklore 16
Philippine history 10, 12, 13, 30, 31, 34, 55, 76, 90, 93, 137, 143, 192
Philippine independence 158
Philippine Legislature 56, 59
Philippine Revolution 158
Philippines XIV, 3, 5, 8, 9, 10, 17, 18, 30, 31, 33, 35, 38, 39, 40, 41, 44, 46, 47, 51, 52, 54, 55, 56, 64, 66, 70, 76, 77, 78, 79, 80, 81, 86, 90, 91, 92, 93, 96, 97, 98, 99, 100, 106, 107, 109, 114, 115, 128, 132, 136, 137, 140, 141, 142, 143, 146, 147, 149, 153, 156, 157, 158, 159, 168, 179, 186, 188, 191, 194, 195, 196, 200, 201, 202, 207
pidgin 109, 160, 162
Pigafetta, Antonio 33
Pilipinas 102, 103, 152, 191
Pilipino 93, 97, 101, 109, 156, 162, 190, 191, 208
Pinoy 41, 90
Pinpin, Tomás 100, 102, 107
PISA survey 108, 109
Plaza Alfonso XII 2, 5, 17, 70, 71, 73, 210
Plaza de Molo 4
Plaza Libertad XIII, 2, 3, 21, 70, 73, 132, 184, 185, 204, 210
Plazoleta Gay XIII, 184
población 4, 11
poems XV, 170, 172, 208
Pope 3, 57, 92, 136
Pope Leo XIII 57
Portuguese 197, 202
Pototan 24, 64, 128, 177, 178
pre-Hispanic 24, 32, 33, 34, 100, 118, 120, 121, 123, 156
Premio Zobel de Hispanidad 208
Prince of Ylongo Poetry 166
principalía 4, 45, 90, 128, 132, 185, 210
Principe Sang Mañga Poeta sa Ylongo 170
Pro Ecclesia et Pontifice medal 3
Protestant 3, 44
Provisional Revolutionary Government of the Visayas and Mindanao 25
Puerto Rico 3, 17, 70, 77, 157, 196
purista XIV, XV, 31, 41, 64, 80, 93, 97, 99, 100, 101, 106, 114, 115, 159, 161, 186, 191
Puti-an Bulabog mountains 26, 27

Q

Qualitative Sociology 40
Queen Isabel 41, 200
Queen Mani-uanti-uan 118
Quezon, President Manuel L. 106

quimonas 24
Quirino administration 6
Quis ut Deus, el brujo rebelde de Yloilo 177

R

racism 38, 40
Rajah Macatunao 118, 121
Rama, Napoleon 99, 109
Recollects 45
Recto, Senator Claro M. 12, 90, 91, 109, 192, 195, 207
Recuerdos de Filipinas 27
refranes 16
renaissance XIII, 195
replicas. XIII
República de Filipinas 7, 8, 18, 32, 46, 52, 53, 71, 72, 86, 160, 178, 190
Republican National Convention 158
revisionist 35, 137, 191
revolucionarios 18, 65, 71
revolution 7, 8, 31, 47, 51, 52, 53, 55, 56, 76, 77, 78, 84, 86, 91, 142, 143
revolutionary 8, 25, 46, 51, 57, 65, 76, 77, 78, 142, 149, 158, 190, 201, 207
Reyes, Fidel A. 98, 160, 211
Rice, Brigadier General Edmund 33
Rivera, José 24, 65, 176, 179
Rivera, Tita Concejo 177
Rivera y Celo, Lourdes 65, 176
Rizal VII, VIII, XIII, 2, 3, 4, 5, 6, 7, 9, 10, 11, 12, 13, 21, 31, 32, 47, 58, 59, 60, 61, 70, 71, 77, 78, 79, 84, 85, 86, 87, 93, 99, 134, 135, 136, 137, 142, 160, 173, 190, 191, 196, 200, 205, 210
Rizal course 12, 86
Rizal, José 2, 21, 31, 47, 70, 71, 77, 84, 134, 137, 142, 196, 205, 210
Rizal, Paciano 6, 142
Robertson, James Alexander 64
Roces, Don Benito 25
Roces, María Luz 25
Rodrigo, Senator Soc 106
Roman Catholic Church 123, 177
Romance Between Sumacuel and Alayon-Capinangan 32
Rome 142
Romuáldez Marcos, President Ferdinand Jr. 205
Rómulo, Carlos P. 77
Roosevelt, President Theodore 40
Root, Elihu 40
Roxas-Ayala clan 78
Roxas, Francisco 77, 78
Royal Audiencia 6, 85
Rueda, Salvador 186
Russia 108, 146

S

Sabah 86
Sacay, Macario 54, 79, 86
Saludes de Camiña Avanceña, Luth 204

Samar 79, 115, 119, 152
San Carlos University 187
San Joaquín 118
San José Parish Church 5
San Juan Bautista Parish Church 193
San Juan del Monte 50, 52, 67, 71
Santa Bárbara 26, 70, 128
Santa Catalina Parish Church 188
Santa Cruz 135
Santarén, Fray Tomás, OSA 34, 119
Santa Rufina 17, 18
Santo Niño 67, 188, 197
Santos, Lope K. 34, 64, 98, 99, 106, 107, 109, 156, 159, 161, 186, 190, 210
Sartorio, Joerem 203
schoolchildren XIV, 32, 35, 51, 64, 67, 84, 86, 106, 159
schoolteachers 20, 27, 102
Schurman Commission 196
Second World War 148, 168, 176
sectarian intolerance 44
Sector de Mestizos 2, 11, 186
Secusana, Aquilino "Quiling" 180

Serafin-Anita Villanueva Arcade XIV
Severino, Tio Emilio 107
Shakira 97
Silay 55, 107
sinamay 84, 135
Sinophobia 41
Sinulog Festival 188
Sison, José María 192
Sisters of Charity 203
SM Mall XIV
Sobre una reseña de Filipinas 84
Sonza, Demetrio 204
sorcerer XIV, 16, 24, 26, 27, 177
sorcery 16, 19, 20
Soriano and Company 202
Sotto, Senator Vicente Sotto y Yap 80, 152
Southeast Asia 52, 110
Soviet-era weapons 146
Spain VII, XIV, 3, 5, 7, 8, 9, 10, 17, 18, 25, 30, 31, 32, 35, 38, 39, 44, 45, 46, 47, 50, 51, 52, 53, 54, 55, 56, 57, 58, 59, 60, 61, 64, 65, 66, 70, 71, 72, 73, 76, 77, 79, 85, 86, 91, 93, 141, 142, 146, 147, 148, 156, 157, 158, 168, 170, 178, 179, 190, 194, 195, 196, 197, 200, 201, 203, 207
Spaniards 9, 10, 16, 25, 30, 40, 41, 44, 45, 50, 55, 57, 64, 65, 66, 71, 77, 78, 122, 128, 147, 159, 167, 186, 197
Spanish VII, VIII, IX, XIII, XIV, XV, 2, 3, 4, 5, 6, 7, 8, 9, 10, 12, 16, 17, 18, 20, 24, 30, 31, 34, 35, 38, 39, 40, 41, 44, 45, 46, 47, 50, 51, 53, 54, 55, 56, 57, 58, 59, 60, 61, 64, 65, 67, 70, 71, 72, 73, 76, 77, 78, 80, 81, 84, 85, 86, 90, 92, 93, 96, 97, 99, 100, 101, 102, 103, 107, 108, 109, 110, 111, 114, 115, 119, 120, 122, 123, 126, 127, 128, 129, 132, 133, 134, 135, 141, 142,

143, 146, 147, 148, 149, 152, 153, 156, 157,
158, 159, 160, 161, 162, 166, 167, 168, 170,
171, 172, 173, 176, 177, 178, 179, 180, 184,
185, 186, 187, 189, 190, 191, 192, 193, 194,
195, 196, 197, 200, 201, 202, 203, 204, 205,
207, 208, 209, 210
Spanish-American War 8, 9, 17, 53, 73, 77, 146, 157
Spanish army 70, 137
Spanish-Binisaya XIII
Spanish colonial government 10
Spanish Constitution of 1812 39
Spanish Cortes 39, 135
Spanish Crown. 38, 41
Spanish era XIII, 184, 202
Spanish language XIII, XIV, 10, 12, 46, 80, 81, 92, 93,
99, 123, 152, 160, 161, 173, 192, 193, 194,
195, 205, 207, 208, 209
Spanishness 38
statehood 38, 40
Steere, Professor Joseph 156
strategic ambiguity 144, 146, 147, 148, 149
sujetos del Rey de España 46
Sulu 122, 123
Sumacuel 32, 118, 119, 166, 167
Sumakwelan 101, 102
Súnico, Hilario 78
Sun Yat Sen High School 180
Supreme Court 41, 50, 98
Syjuco, Judy Jalbuena 25
Syjuco, Miguel 25

T

Taal 31, 65, 72, 120, 121
Tabucan Bridge 184
Tabugón 17, 18, 176, 177, 178, 180
Tabuwanay 122
Tagalog XIV, XV, 5, 7, 8, 25, 30, 31, 32, 34, 35, 41,
44, 46, 47, 50, 53, 55, 71, 72, 76, 79, 84, 90,
91, 93, 97, 99, 100, 101, 102, 103, 106, 107,
108, 109, 114, 115, 120, 152, 153, 158, 159,
162, 163, 167, 173, 180, 190, 191, 192, 208
Taglish 109, 160, 162, 187
Taiwan 146, 149
Taiwanese 146
Taiwan Strait 146
Talisay 55, 132
Tanza 184
Tanza seashore 184
Taruc, Luis 192
Tayabas 47
Tejero, Henry C. 204
teniente del barrio 16
Teniente Guimó VII, XIV, 16, 17, 18, 19, 20, 21, 24,
25, 26, 27, 177
Teodoro, Professor Luis V. 98
tertulias de la semana 132
The Battle of Batangas 65
The Daily Guardian 98
The Day the Dancers Stayed: Performing in the Filipino/

American Diaspora 147
The Masons 3, 77
The Roots of the Filipino Nation 55, 57
Thomasite 99
Tigbauan 204
Tinocuan 18, 24
Toledo 41
Tondo 61, 77
Torre, Serapión 170, 171
totalitarian history 35
Treaty of Paris XIV, 8, 17, 18, 25, 55, 71, 157
Trece Mártires 77
Treñas, Mayor Jerry XIII
Tribunal de Guerra 71
Tupas, Governor Neil XIII

U

Ukraine 146
United States II, XIII, 7, 8, 18, 20, 30, 35, 38, 40, 41,
46, 47, 70, 71, 77, 90, 97, 108, 141, 146, 157,
158, 176, 179, 196
University of Michigan 156, 157
University of San Agustín 180, 204, 211
University of Santo Tomás 24, 61, 84, 92
University of the Philippines 98, 107, 192, 200
University of Valencia 97
U.S. 7, 8, 17, 21, 33, 38, 47, 51, 53, 54, 56, 59, 64, 70,
98, 106, 109, 114, 141, 142, 146, 147, 148,
149, 152, 156, 178, 179, 196, 210
USAFFE. See also United States Army Forces Far East
20, 176, 187
U.S. Congress 98, 149
U.S. military 33
USS Baltimore 18, 21
USS Petrel 18, 21, 47, 76

V

Valenzuela, Pio 137
Valladolid 200
Vamenta, Representative Isidro 193
Venezuela 202
Vermont 156
verso de arte mayor 170
verso romance. 168
Vidal, Gore Vidal 46
Vietnam 45
Vigan 110, 204
Villa de Arévalo VIII, 126, 127, 129, 185, 204
Villanueva de Vargas, Teresa 202
Villanueva y Felipe, Emilio 2, 6
Villanueva y Gonzalo, Francisco "Frank" 200
Villaruel, Rosario 85
Villegas y Soldi, Lieutenant General Pantaleón. See also
León Kilát. 8, 78, 79
Visayan VIII, 3, 35, 53, 55, 64, 79, 80, 107, 115, 119,
126, 127, 132, 142, 148, 162, 172, 176, 177,
180, 191, 192, 194, 195, 197, 200, 208, 209
Visayas XIII, 20, 25, 32, 35, 50, 55, 61, 64, 65, 70, 79,

110, 115, 184, 190, 192, 193, 197, 201, 208
vocabulary XIV, 100, 102
Voluntarios XIV, 8, 17, 18, 32, 35, 47, 50, 53, 54, 64, 65, 70, 71, 72, 73, 76, 78, 79, 86, 115, 146, 148, 186, 190

Zaragoza Cano, Flavio 34, 109, 111, 115, 167, 170, 171, 208, 211
zarzuelas, 6, 169
Zobel 193, 195, 208
Zozobrado, Ofelia 188

W

Walled City of Intramuros 148
war 3, 6, 7, 8, 9, 17, 18, 19, 35, 46, 47, 51, 52, 55, 56, 61, 64, 70, 72, 73, 142, 147, 149, 152, 158, 159, 160, 176, 179, 196
war atrocities 9
Warsaw Pact 146
WB. 187. See also World Bank
Webster's Dictionary 34
West, Barbara A. 156
Western XIII, XIV, 40, 61, 110, 201, 208
Western Visayas XIII, 110, 201
West Philippine Sea 149
White Anglo-Saxon Protestant 3
White, Janet Frances II
Windham de Gómez, Dolores 6
Windham, Guillermo 6
witchcraft 16
Worcester. See Dean C. Worcester. 64, 66, 67, 79, 84, 98, 99, 100, 101, 102, 103, 109, 114, 156, 157, 158, 159, 160, 161, 186, 196, 197, 210, 211
World Bank XIV, 102, 108. See also WB
World War II 134
Wyndham, William 6

X

xenophobia 40

Y

Yabes, Professor Leopoldo 192
Yap-Sandiego Ancestral House 189, 190
Yap Sandiego, Valentino 188
Ybiernas, Don Vicente 20, 132. 133
Ylongo II, V, VIII, IX, XI, XIII, XIV, 6, 9, 16, 18, 21, 24, 26, 27, 32, 33, 34, 35, 50, 53, 54, 64, 65, 67, 70, 71, 72, 76, 78, 80, 86, 91, 96, 97, 101, 102, 107, 114, 115, 119, 120, 123, 128, 132, 133, 134, 162, 166, 167, 169, 170, 171, 172, 173, 178, 180, 185, 186, 190, 200, 201, 204, 207, 208
Ylongo-Hiligaynon V, XIII, XIV
Ylongo poetry. 169, 170, 172
Ylongo-Quinaray-a 119
Ynchausti Commercial House 4
Yreñeta, José 176
Yulo, Governor José 203
Yusay-Consing residence 11

Z

Zamboanga 18, 70, 71, 73, 76, 96, 111

www.ingramcontent.com/pod-product-compliance
Lightning Source LLC
Chambersburg PA
CBHW020354170426
43200CB00005B/160